THE AFFIRMING FLAME

The Affirming Flame

RELIGION, LANGUAGE, LITERATURE

By David Patterson

University of Oklahoma Press: Norman and London

BL
65
L2
P38
1988

ABV- 3014

6/1988
Ref

By David Patterson

Faith and Philosophy (Washington, D.C., 1982)
(Translator) *Confession,* by Leo Tolstoy (New York, 1983)
(Translator) *The Forged Coupon,* by Leo Tolstoy (New York, 1984)
(Translator) *Diary of a Superfluous Man,* by Ivan Turgenev (New York, 1984)
The Way of the Child (Houston, 1988)
(Translator) *Winter Notes on Summer Impressions,* by F. M. Dostoevsky (Evanston, Ill., 1988)
The Affirming Flame (Norman, 1988)

Library of Congress Cataloging-in-Publication Data

Patterson, David.
   The affirming flame: religion, language, literature / by David Patterson.—1st ed.
   p. cm.
   Bibliography: p.
   Includes index.
   ISBN 0-8061-2109-2 (alk. paper)
   1. Languages—Religious aspects.   2. Religion and literature.
I. Title.
BL65.L2P38   1988
200—dc19   87-30026
                                                                CIP

The paper in this book meets the guidelines for permanence and durability of the Committee on Production Guidelines for Book Longevity of the Council on Library Resources, Inc.

Copyright © 1988 by the University of Oklahoma Press, Norman, Publishing Division of the University. Manufactured in the U.S.A. First edition.

FOR MY PARENTS

Contents

Preface   ix

1. Opening Remarks: Why Religion, Language,
   Literature?   3

Part One: Literary Logos and Literary Criticism   19

2. The Johannine Logos and Literary Criticism   21
3. Lacan's *Parole* and the Literary Critic   37
4. Dostoevsky's *Dvoinik* per Lacan's *Parole*   58

Part Two: Religious Concepts of Language and
         Literature   75

5. Mikhail Bakhtin and the Dialogical Dimensions of
   the Novel   77
6. The Apotheosis of Presence: Buber, Wiesel, and
   Hasidism   93

Part Three: Messianic Elements of Language and
           Literature   115

7. Messianic Aspects of the Child in the Works of
   Elie Wiesel   117

8. Paltiel's Quest for the Messiah in Wiesel's *The
    Testament*   135
9. Conclusion   152

Notes   159
Select Bibliography   169
Index   173

Preface

In these chapters I attempt to develop a few strands of thought to establish some integration and interrelation of religion, language, and literature. Focusing on the selected particulars represented in this volume, I set out to offer the reader a general sense of the religious dimensions of language and literature, the linguistic elements of religion and literature, and the literary aspects of religion and language. The religious tradition I draw most upon is Judeo-Christian, and I draw upon only a small portion of that tradition. If it seems that I indulge in a curious interplay of Judaism and Christianity and at times lump some of their ideas together, it is because I am more concerned with how they are joined according to the spirit than with how they are separated according to the letter.

I harbor no illusions about the distance between the vast horizons of this book's subject and the modest scope of its treatment. At best, I but scratch a few surfaces. My hope, however, is that in scratching those surfaces I may plant some seeds that will grow and thus bring something up from the depths and into the light. As for the soil in which these seeds are planted, philosophers of religion, philosophers of language, literary critics, and literary theorists might find these chapters of interest. Certainly among the people in my audience will be those who have a concern for the ties that bind religion, language, and literature, and that could include a good number and variety of thinkers. To be sure, the three areas cited in the book's title pervade our intellectual, spiritual, and emotional existence; for religion is the soul, language the substance, and literature the song of life.

Finally, on a formal note, it should be pointed out that, unless indicated otherwise, all translations are my own. I would also like gratefully to acknowledge two periodicals, which published earlier versions of two of the chapters in this book. Chapter 4 is based on the article "Dostoevsky's *Dvoinik* per Lacan's *Parole,*" which appeared in *Essays in Literature,* 10 (Fall 1983), 299–307, and Chapter 5 is based on "Mikhail Bakhtin and the Dialogical Dimensions of the Novel," which was published in the *Journal of Aesthetics and Art Criticism,* 44 (Winter 1985), 131–39.

DAVID PATTERSON

Stillwater, Oklahoma

THE AFFIRMING FLAME

CHAPTER ONE

Opening Remarks: Why Religion, Language, Literature?

TO ESTABLISH SOME FOOTING with respect to the matter at hand, I should begin by addressing the point of this endeavor: Why religion, language, literature? Such a question, however, harbors several questions, which may be rendered in a number of ways. How, for example, do religion and literature arise, how are they related, and what does language have to do with them? Then, of course, there is the question why we bother with these notions at all: What is our stake in religion, language, and literature?

Definitions and Origins

One way to begin is to attempt a definition of what we are talking about; and if we begin with the first term, perhaps it will lead us to the other two. What, then, do we mean by religion? Ludwig Feuerbach puts it simply—or perhaps not so simply—by declaring, "True bliss in life is true religion."[1] Making use of bigger words, if not bigger concepts, Miguel de Unamuno argues that "the very essence of all religion" turns on "the problem of human destiny, of eternal life, or of the human finality of the Universe and of God"; this problem, moreover, Unamuno renders as a "religious longing for union with God" that can be consummated "only in life."[2] In still another example, Henri Bergson defines religion as "that element which is called upon to make good

3

any deficiency of attachment to life"; and "attachment to life," he goes on to say, is inseparable from "this principle, joy in joy, love for that which is all love."[3] The quality that makes all of these statements definitions of religion is their accent on life: religion concerns a relation to that which is both within and beyond life. It entails a process of bonding, of connecting one thing with another—life with life, the human with the divine.

When that relation becomes problematic, when the "deficiency of attachment to life" arises, so does religion. And with religion comes literature, or at least the seeds of literature, in the form of myth. The religious longing for relation initially finds its expression in myth, so that religion begets myth and not myth religion; in the words of Bergson, "Religion is what accounts for the myth-making function: faculty standing to religion in the relationship of effect and not of cause" (pp. 108–109). Religion accounts for the literature-making function, for the poetic utterance "thou art that," which joins life to life when instead of a bond there is only a void. Like life itself, religion and literature are, in a sense, created out of nothingness. This stance toward the origin of religion and literature is suggested in *The Masks of God: Primitive Mythology,* in which Joseph Campbell concludes that myth is

> conceived, like all poetry, in depth, but susceptible of interpretation on various levels. The shallowest minds see in it the local scenery; the deepest, the foreground of the void; and between are all the stages of the Way from the ethnic to the elementary idea, the local to the universal being, which is Everyman, as he both knows and is afraid to know.[4]

Conceived in language, the myth that Campbell says we "see" is also something that we hear. To borrow a phrase from Susan Handelman, "Vision is hearing the word."[5] And what is it that we perceive? The bond that religion seeks and literature voices.

As word is joined to word, subject to predicate, text to interpretation—so is life attached to life, the human to the divine. It is no accident that for the Yahwists "literature provided the one form in which Yahweh could be envisioned," as Herbert Schneidau has pointed out. "All other forms, including the shrines, the priesthood, and the rituals themselves, were suspect. Thus the Hebrews became the People of the Book, an attribution that has some bearing on the provenance of literature in the West."[6] It will also be recalled that on the Hebraic view everything comes into being by virtue of the word, or *davhar,* which is "an aspect of the continuous divine creative force itself," as Handelman explains. It "is not simply *thing . . .* but also *action, efficacious fact, event, matter, process*" (p. 32). In the Hebraic tradition, when literature arises as an expression of religious longing, there also arises an involvement with language. The attachment to life that religion seeks is also an attachment to the word as it unfolds in a literary text. Hence Schneidau declares:

> The Bible's "influence" is not to give us genres or archetypes which can be endlessly refilled with extraneous materials; instead it plays a role which demands that we acknowledge how precarious is our grasp of any meaning in the world at all and that we force ourselves to probe the words and forms before us in a never-ending labor. Like the dynamic incompleteness of language itself, the gap or lack that gives it an endless, never-catching-up-to-itself character, the Bible sets the problem of retracing urgent but unfixable messages, located in a series of texts which come to no real end or conclusion. Writing posits the original disjunction, a violent removal from the immediacy of meaning. [P. 255]

Out of language itself—the language of literature, which is a form of writing—come both the problem and the solution addressed by religion as well as by literature. The ground is no sooner laid than it crumbles, and the longing for the relation that characterizes religion leads us to rediscover in language the power to heal the wound.

Without the rupture that is writing, neither religion nor literature can happen. To paraphrase Harold Bloom, a poem's meaning is its moaning (see Handelman, p. 189), and the origin of outcry is the origin of religion, language, and literature. They live inasmuch as they are threatened, their life accentu-

ated by its proximity to death. At once blinded by presence
and haunted by absence, writing—*écriture,* or Scripture, to
use Jacques Derrida's term—is "the principle of death and
difference in the becoming of being."[7] If the impetus toward
life's attachment to life instills the language that is literature
with its religious dimension, so too does the detachment from
life of death and difference. Attachment is defined by detachment; presence is posited by absence. Religion seeks the sign
that will link the human to the divine, and so the text of signs
constituting literature is born. The bond, however, also becomes a barrier. "The sign," Derrida reminds us, "is always
the sign of the Fall. Absence always relates to distance from
God" (p. 401). The distance from God is precisely what col-
lapses the distance between religion, language, and literature.
They arise together in a time of detachment, and the time is
always now, the place forever east of Eden.

The Destitute Time

The destitute time is more than a time of fashion, fad, and
cleverness in critical inquiry, more than a time overshadowed
by a sky transformed into a cemetery for six million dead.
Time itself is destitute. To live in time is to live on the edge of
the *not yet,* a position that announces the deficiency of attachment to life. It is not simply the next moment that is *not yet*
but the ultimate Word of Truth that is *not yet.* Here lies an
important *why* in our concern with religion, language, and literature, an important stake in dealing with these notions. The
destitute time is the time of religion, language, and literature,
the time when the human being's relation to the word that generates the attachment to life is in question.
   In the essay "What Are Poets for?" Martin Heidegger
writes, "To be a poet in a destitute time means: to attend,
singing, to the trace of the fugitive gods."[8] Attending entails
an effort to generate a relation through the process of listening
and response. Summoning itself, language is the singing, literature the song, and the song life. Like the voice of the muse

resounding through the poet—a voice that comes both from him and from beyond him—language works through literature to fetch the trace of the fugitive gods from the abyss. The destitute time is the age of the abyss; we stand on one shore while life recedes to the other. And that abyss, that Open, as Heidegger calls it, is just where the poet must venture, by means of his song, if he is to regain a bond with the fugitive gods and, thus, with life.

Elie Wiesel tells us that when Rebbe Hersh, son of Hasidism's founder, the Baal Shem, asked his father in a dream how to serve God, "the Baal Shem climbed a high mountain and threw himself into the abyss. 'Like this,' he answered."[9] And so it is with serving the Word and embracing life. Only when all pretentious shields and protective barriers have been removed is it possible to leap into the Open to affirm life; only by leaving behind the idle talk of calculation and negotiation can one draw the breath more daring by a breath, which is poetry. Nikos Kazantzakis may give a hint of what it is like in the Open:

> "We tremble. We guess what a frightening abyss lies beneath us. In the distance we can hear the noise of the other leaves of the tremendous tree, we feel the sap rising from the roots to our leaf and our hearts swell. Bent thus over the awe-inspiring abyss, with all our bodies and all our souls, we tremble with terror. From that moment begins . . ."
>
> I stopped. I wanted to say "from that moment begins poetry," but Zorba would not have understood. I stopped.
>
> "What begins?" asked Zorba's anxious voice. "Why did you stop?"
>
> ". . . begins the great danger, Zorba. Some grow dizzy and delirious, others are afraid."[10]

Poetry: the great danger, the thing we work for in fear and trembling. Its language, the sap of the great tree, brings us out of the fortress we disguise as a home and draws us into the temple, "the precinct (*templum*)" (Heidegger, *Poetry,* p. 132), of life. The literary language of poetry *is* the temple of life, for it is the language of affirmation, of yea-saying, uttered in a time when saying yes is most difficult. W. H. Auden issues a summons to affirmation despite the destitute time in his poem "In Memory of W. B. Yeats" when he writes:

> Follow, poet, follow right
> To the bottom of the night,
> With your unconstraining voice
> Still persuade us to rejoice.[11]

Once again we see the venture into the abyss, "to the bottom of the night," from which the flame of affirmation must be fetched.

To the extent that religion is a seeking, it is also a saying, an effort to speak the salvific word. In this attempt to speak, in the saying rather than in the said, lies affirmation. Saying, as Emmanuel Levinas describes it, is "a sign of this giving of signs, that is, of this non-indifference, a sign of this impossibility of slipping away and being replaced, of this identity, this uniqueness: here I am."[12] In the flame of passion about to explode, language itself speaks, making a sign of itself and proclaiming the *here* by which I am. Drawing the breath about to be transformed into the Word, we shudder. The armor that encumbers and the walls that imprison disappear; we tumble "into the heights," as Heidegger puts it, "the heights which open up a depth."[13] Like Daedalus ascending from his prison into the heavens, the affirming flame rises to overcome the beleaguering gravity of the destitute time. The leap into the Open takes the human being not outward but upward, soaring inward, to what Rainer Maria Rilke calls "the depth dimension of our inner being" (see Heidegger, *Poetry,* p. 128). This is the place to which literature takes poet and reader, the realm opened up by the literary Word; this is where religion is fulfilled, where its joy in joy and love for love abide. The inner being that Rilke refers to is the source of life, which is occluded in the destitute time. The walls of the already said, which insulate us from life, insolate us from the source of life, and it is literature's saying that moves toward the source and instills it with an ever-increasing depth.

Religion, language, and literature come together in this movement, propelled by the passion of love, the flame of affirmation, and the beckoning of the Word—from the beginning. "With the drawing of this Love and the voice of this Calling," T. S. Eliot writes, we "arrive where we started." [14] The movement of religion, language, and literature is a movement of return, and the need to return is the sign of the destitute time. The religious accent on return can be found, for example, in the prophets Isaiah (44:22), Jeremiah (3:22), Hosea (6:1), and Joel (2:12)—all of whom are voices crying in the wilderness of a destitute time. The return to Yahweh summoned by these prophets is a return to the Word; "Hear the word of the Lord," says Isaiah, "ye that tremble at his word" (66:5). For in the destitute time the Word itself is in exile, divorced from its meaning. When the Word is in exile, words are just for noise, substitutions for reality, bought and sold by the merchants who have invaded the temple. The return to the beginning, to the source, is a return to the Word that was in the beginning, to the Word by which life comes to life. "Our Redeemer is your ancient name," Isaiah declares (63:16).

The beginning is not the beginning of time; rather, it is the thing lost in the destitute time. It does not lie in the remote past; instead, it is the eternal time of creation, forever at the threshold of language. "The threshold of language," Michel Foucault tells us, "lies at the point where the verb first appears. This verb must therefore be treated as a composite entity, at the same time a word among other words. . . . It is on the fringe of discourse, at the connection between what is said and what is saying itself." [15] Through the words we utter and the silences that frame them, we move along the edge of the Word and live in its creation; lying on the fringe of discourse, the Word spoken in the beginning speaks from the beginning. "In taking a single word by assault," Wiesel has written, "it is possible to discover the secret of creation, the center where all the threads come together." [16] Drawing its spirit from religion, literature endeavors to penetrate the secret of creation; drawing his breath from language, the poet takes the Word by assault. As the Word is wrestled from language, life is wrenched from the destitute time; that which had been detached and dismembered is re-membered, made hale, whole, and holy. Creating through the Word, the poet participates in the saying of the creation and pronounces it to be very good. The summons to which the poet responds calls forth by calling back. The Voice asks for a messenger in a destitute time, and the poet answers, "Here I am: send me" (cf. Isa. 6:8–9).

If the problem of the destitute time is a problem of response, it is also one of hearing. The religious longing for attachment to life and the literary effort to voice the longing constitute a struggle to speak that is also a struggle to hear. In the words of Heidegger: "Man speaks to the extent that he responds to language. This response is a hearing" (*Unterwegs*, pp. 32–33). Hearing comes by the word. The poet who assails the Word through his voice strains to hear the Word that enlightens and the call that awakens. Thus Isaiah cries, "Hear, and your soul shall live" (55:3); for to hear is to attend, and to attend is to be present. Again, presence is generated through the inhaling and exhaling of hearing and response, through the struggle to bespeak and burn with the affirming flame. Only in affirmation is the self *here;* in despair the self is always somewhere else. Religion, language, and literature are of one piece in the effort to hear the summons and respond, "Here I am." This is the project of affirmation common to poet and prophet, both called in the destitute time. Each is the *nabi,* for "with the *nabi,* writes Martin Buber, "something descends from the divine sphere upon man: *dabhar* or *ruah, logos* or *pneuma,* word or spirit." [17] The Word or spirit that descends from the divine spirit—from language—voices the affirmation and is the vessel of presence.

The destitute time is a time of loss, a time of being lost. Once more, the time is always now, the project forever at hand; as José Ortega y Gasset has pointed out, "Man feels himself lost not merely from time to time but all the time, or, what is the same thing, . . . man consists in substance of feeling himself lost." [18] Attending to the trace of the fugitive gods, the poet attempts to fetch the lost word from the divine sphere. Yet, in a sense, the divine sphere is not someplace else or in another world. In the words of Eliot:

If the lost word is lost, if the spent word is spent,
If the unheard, unspoken
Word is unspoken, unheard;
Still is the unspoken word, the Word unheard,
The Word without a word, the Word within
The world and for the world.[19]

The project of relation is to be *here,* not hereafter; life must find its attachment to *this* life if it is to have meaning. Heidegger has said that "where the word fails, so does the thing" (*Unterwegs,* p. 163). A stronger statement can now be made: where religion, language, and literature fail so does meaning. The creation of meaning—and, through meaning, affirmation—is the pressing *why* of religion, language, and literature.

The Creation of Meaning

At this point what Bergson and Unamuno have said about religion should be recalled. Bergson places the accent on life's attachment to life, while Unamuno invokes the religious longing for union with God. In one thought is the suggestion of a relation between lives, as between two human beings, and in the other a relation to a Third, to God. The creation of meaning entails both relations; it is an event that occurs *between* human and human and between human and God. From the standpoint of religion, language, and literature, the relation to another person always includes a relation to a Third, to what Jacques Lacan calls the Other with a capital *O* when he says: "The Other with a big O is the scene of the Word insofar as the scene of the Word is always in third position between two subjects. This is only in order to introduce the dimension of Truth."[20] The realm of truth is the realm of meaning, and the role of religion, language, and literature in the creation of meaning is to establish a relation to truth. It is the place where, in Mikhail Bakhtin's words, we encounter "the overman, the over-*I,* that is, the witness and judge of every man (of every *I*)."[21] The Other is the witness—the implied reader, as it were—of every undertaking of religion, language, and litera-

ture and of every response to them, including this one. And
the creation of meaning rests on the relation of the human
being to that witness.

The creation of meaning, then, is an answering to the Word
that makes meaning possible, thus meeting what Bakhtin regards as a special responsibility:

> Wherever the alibi becomes a prerequisite for creation and expres-
> sion there can be no responsibility, no seriousness, no significance.
> A special responsibility is required . . . ; but this responsibility
> can be founded only on a profound belief in a higher truth, . . .
> the belief that another, higher being responds to my special re-
> sponsibility, that I do not act in an utter void. Apart from this
> belief there can be only empty pretense. [P. 179]

The appeal to a higher being is a distinguishing feature of both
religious and literary utterance; it is the tie that binds religion,
language, and literature in their effort to create meaning. Wiesel
makes this point when he writes that "prayer and literature, both
of them, take hold of mundane words and confer upon them another sense; both raise an appeal to that which, within man, is
the most personal and most elevated of needs." [22] Reading "the
most personal and most elevated of needs," we recall once
more Unamuno's allusion to the religious longing for God.
From that longing comes the appeal that characterizes the language of religion and literature. To confer, through the Word,
another sense upon the Word implies a creative aspect of the
Word itself. Indeed, such a view is in keeping with the Hebraic
notion of the word, or *davhar*. In this connection, Handelman
points out that, although *davhar* means both *word* and *thing*,

> *reality* is a far more appropriate word to use than *thing*, for it does
> not evoke the same connotations as do *substance* and *being*. Of
> course, the physical object itself was not considered to be identical
> to the word which designated it, but for the Hebrew mind, the
> essential reality of the table was the word of God, not any idea of
> the table as in the Platonic view, or some *ousia*. The Hebrew word
> was not just an arbitrary designation, but an aspect of the continu-
> ous divine creative force itself. [P. 32]

Only by construing the Word in these terms can the creation of meaning become a task—*the* task—of religion, language, and literature.

Regarding the Word as an aspect of the divine creative force bears another implication for the creation of meaning: it points to what Bakhtin describes as "the totality of all meaningful significance and direction in life" (p. 98). This is Bakhtin's definition of spirit, which is very much like Lacan's notion of the Other. The creation of meaning is the creation of a relation to spirit and the affirmation of a spiritual relation to life. This is another important expression of the *why* of religion, language, and literature and of our concern with them. Just as religion and literature make language into a response to spirit, so must we respond to religion and literature, seeking the spirit in the midst of the text. Recall, for example, the words of the old abbott in Kazantzakis's *The Last Temptation of Christ:* "You open the prophets and your eyes are able to see nothing but the letters. But what can the letters say? They are the black bars of the prison where the spirit strangles itself with screaming. Between the letters and the lines, and all around the blank margins, the spirit circulates freely." [23] The task of religion, language and literature poses a like task for the one who stands before a text; interpretation is not so much a reaction *to* the text as a relation *with* the text. And inasmuch as it is a relation with the text, it is part of the life of the text. Thus author and commentator are both engaged in the effort to create meaning and affirm life. The house of both the poet and the Jew, Handelman has noted, "is a sacred text in the middle of commentaries," adding that "Barthes would probably substitute the word *critic* for *poet* here. In his (Rabbinic) words, 'the book creates meaning; the meaning creates life'" (p. 81). The meaning affirms life—again, the *why* of religion, language, and literature.

Substituting the word *critic* for *poet,* we see that the book's endeavor to create meaning entails a response to its "sacred text." Meaning lies not in the fixed forms of the already said, in the imprint on the page, but in the process of dialogical interaction with the Word. Our interest in religion, language, and literature, then, is not only a concern with *what* they are but also a concern with *how* we are related to them. For in this relation lies the attachment to life and, therefore, any meaning life may have. "The crucial recognitions here," writes Handelman, "are that the text is a 'production' and not a 'representation' of meaning, and that the goal of literature is to make the reader a producer of texts" (pp. 79–80). The goal of literature, in other words, is to engage the reader in the responsive creation of meaning and affirmation of life, to draw the reader into the play of language and into the passion of religious longing. This play and this passion—this *interplay* of religion, language, and literature—characterize the process of becoming that Bakhtin associates with spiritual life when he says:

> The definition given to me lies not in the categories of temporal being but in the categories of the *not-yet-existing,* in the categories of purpose and meaning, in the meaningful future, which is at odds with anything I have in the past or present. To be myself for myself means yet becoming myself (*to cease becoming myself . . . means spiritual death*). [P. 109]

The yet-to-be lies in the still-outstanding, the forever unuttered, the ultimate Word that is "there," in a third position, in dialogical interaction. And wherever response and interpretation are dialogical, they are spiritual.

Viewing the Word as spirit or along spiritual lines, I place myself forever on the threshold, at the critical zero point, where I encounter the *not yet* of the process of becoming. This is where religious longing is transformed into literary text, where deep calls to deep, in the Word's effort to confer a new sense upon itself. The new sense is the renewed attachment of life to life, the union between human being and human being, between human being and God. If religion continually addresses the "deficiency of attachment to life," language is the house of that address; and literature, the text aflame with affirmation, is the product and progenitor of religion and language. Thus, suggesting a correction of Plato's division of knowledge into separate categories, religion, language, and literature merge to form not a new category but a single event: the creation of meaning through affirmation.

The Merging of the Categories

In *The Slayers of Moses,* Susan Handelman relates the following episode from the Avodah Zarah Talmud:

> When the Romans came to take R. Hanina ben Teradion to be burned to death for teaching Torah despite their prohibition, they found him in the act of reading the Torah. As they took him, his daughter began to weep, and he questioned her why. She answered, "I weep for the Torah that is to be burned with you." He answered, "The Torah is fire, and no fire can burn fire itself." They seized him and wrapped him in the scroll of the Torah, heaped faggots around him and lit the pyre. In the moment of his agony, his disciples asked him, "Rabbi, what do you see?" He replied: "I see the parchment consumed by fire, but the letters of the Scriptures are flying upwards." [P. 178]

Who could conjure a more stirring image of the affirming flame? Here the linkage between religion and language is graphic and clear. And the tale itself is literature.

Contrary to what some thinkers maintain, we can now recognize that religion is much closer to literature than to theology,* anthropology, sociology, psychology, or other systematic disciplines. Its concern, like that of literature, lies not with speculation but with revelation, not with system but with spirit. It is no coincidence that texts such as the Bible, the Koran, the Bhagavad Gita, and the Tao te-ching contain more tale and poetry than critique and treatise. The connection between religion's sacred text and literature's extension of that text has also been established, whether the response is undertaken by poet or by critic. The thing that joins religion and literature is the Word as spirit, which abides in language.

---

*Here a distinction between religion and theology should be made. By *theology* I mean the activity of systematizing a set of principles concerning the nature of God, points of doctrine, and so on. By *religion* I have in mind the lived process of creating meaning and affirming life, Bergson's "joy in joy" and "love for that which is all love."

Thus we have a first glimpse of the rationale behind this treatment of religion, language, and literature and the issues that draw them together. At this point a few questions emerge: What, for example, does regarding the Word as spirit imply about how we view literature? What is literature's capacity for dealing with the religious dimension of life? And what impact may literature have on a human being's relation to God and to fellow human beings? In an effort to respond to these questions, I have divided this book into three parts: Literary Logos and Literary Response, Religious Concepts of Language and Literature, and Messianic Elements of Language and Literature. The chapters in each part support my general thesis that literature is essential to religious life, for the language of literature—poetic language—is the language of the spirit.

As for the individual chapters, chapter 2 proceeds from Saint John's concept of God as word and as spirit to examine the implications of his thinking for the reader's relation to the literary text. I argue that Saint John's approach to the logos (which is distinguished from the classical concept of logos) points the way to something more than a strictly aesthetic or formal treatment of literature. Literature is not an object of observation or detached commentary; rather, it is a voice that beckons the reader to create a meaningful presence before the text by generating a personal, dialogical, and even passionate relation to the text. Considered in the light of the Johannine logos, the literary text puts the same question to the critic that God put to the first man: Where are you? The third chapter adds to the second by arguing that, just as the psychoanalytic subject faces the task of achieving relation through the word (Lacan's *parole*), so does the literary critic. The opposite of the *parole* is the -ism, and those who bring to a text the baggage of a predetermined discourse—Marxist, formalist, structuralist, deconstructionist, or whatever—fail to create a response of their own. Instead, the -ism speaks for them and thus displaces them. Offering an example of a Lacanian approach to a literary text, chapter 4 examines Fyodor Dostoevsky's *Dvoinik* (The Double) in the light of Lacan's *parole*. Here I consider what Dostoevsky's novel reveals about the interplay of presence and absence that is central to Lacan.

The chapters in part two address the dialogical dimensions of literature in relation to the spiritual dimensions of literature, with language crucial to both. Here I examine the dialogical word conceived as the spiritual word. The first chapter in part two (chapter 5) investigates Mikhail Bakhtin's approach to the novel as a dialogical, and therefore spiritual, literary form with a religious stake in the pursuit of truth. According to Bakhtin, the novel underscores a dialogical presence in life, a presence characterized by the interrelation of speaking and response. Chapter 6 examines a philosophical figure and a literary figure—Martin Buber and Elie Wiesel—and their approach to Hasidism. The two agree that on the Hasidic view the accent is on presence and that presence is rooted in the Word, a position that lends a philosophical element to Wiesel's literature and a literary facet to Buber's philosophy. Wiesel, however, deals with Hasidism by the light of the flames of the Holocaust and thus confronts religious questions that elude Buber.

Pursuing further a consideration of Wiesel—a poet operating in our own destitute time—part three explores a single theme in his writings as well as a single work. Chapter 7 explores the messianic elements of the child in Wiesel's literature, while chapter 8 considers the main character's quest for the Messiah in Wiesel's *The Testament*. This is where the issue of literature's impact on our relation to God and to one another comes into focus, since these chapters examine literature's revelation of the Messiah and the redemptive value of its quest for rebirth. Here lies the ultimate support for my thesis concerning literature's relation to religious life and the spiritual essence of literature. More important, we discover in part three the stake in setting forth the thesis. For here we see what it means to dance, though the ground has crumbled from under our feet, what it is like to resurrect some attachment to life from the ashes of life's destruction, and what is entailed in the embrace of joy in joy and love of love when rejoicing and loving must be sufficient unto themselves. What is at stake,

then, is the ability to burn with an affirming flame, to hear and
to heed the poet's cry of affirmation as uttered in Auden's
"September 1, 1939":

> May I, composed like them
> Of Eros and of dust,
> Beleaguered by the same
> Negation and despair,
> Show an affirming flame.
> [P. 537]

The why of religion, language, and literature? To create joyful
love and loving joy, to fuel the flame of affirmation. Others
might say it is to create spirit. But that is the same thing.

PART ONE

Literary Logos and Literary Criticism

THE DIALOGICAL WORD instills literature with a religious dimension; the dialogical word is precisely the literary word. To provide a basis for this idea, part one begins by establishing a critical approach to literature. And it is an *approach,* a movement rather than a method, by which the critic endeavors to generate a personal, responsive relation to the literary text. It is relation, grounded in the dialogical word, that brings the individual into contact with the religious dimensions of literature.

The bonds that link religion, language, and literature are circular. While the approach to literature presented in part one begins outside the normally delineated confines of literature, the religious concept of language and the Word outlined in chapter 2, on the Johannine logos, may be found within literature itself. Indeed, much of the Gospel of Saint John is poetry written to give voice to a religious idea as only poetry can. Chapter 3, "Lacan's *Parole* and the Literary Critic," begins further outside literature but moves further inside the relation between word and presence. Just as the religious undertaking is to become present in relation to the Word, so the critical undertaking is to become present in relation to the literary text. The critical process itself, then, has a religious dimension, which is constituted by the language of relation; this language consists of a dialogue with the text and, through the text, with oneself. Finally, chapter 4, on Dostoevsky's *Dvoi-*

19

nik, offers an example of the critical approach set forth, dealing with the issues surrounding word and presence within a literary work.

Part one is thus intended to show that literary logos—the literary Word—is a presence or a force that distinguishes the religious aspects of literature and the critic's response to literature. While the critical reaction to music or art does not consist of composing or painting, the literary critic must respond in kind, in the same medium, answering the summons of the Word by giving voice to the Word. Saint Augustine once said that when we behold God in the world, it is God who sees through our eyes. In a similar way, when we address the literary logos through critical response, it is the logos that speaks through us.

CHAPTER TWO

The Johannine Logos and Literary Criticism

THE GREEK TERM *logos* may be translated as "reckoning," "explanation," "reason," "saying," "word," and so on; in more general terms, logos is at once a thought and the expression of the thought, simultaneously an idea and the manifestation of the idea. In the philosophy of Plato the logos is associated with the concept of *eikon,* or image, an intermediary between the ideal and the sensible worlds. The Greek notion found its way into Hebrew scholarship through the work of Philo Judaeus, a contemporary of Jesus. Philo regarded the logos as the revelation of divine reason or wisdom, which draws the human being into a relationship with God; it is the person's access to the logos, on Philo's view, that makes him the image of God. All genuine wisdom that one might acquire is the image of God's wisdom and unites the human with the divine. The logos in this case is not precisely the Word but is rather the mirror by which divine reason is reflected in human reason, better understood as a principle than as a living entity.

The connection between the logos and the Word as a living being perhaps has deeper roots in Judaic tradition than in Greek philosophy. A poetic personification of the Word of God is found in a number of Scriptures. For example: "The Word is very near to you" (Deut. 30:14); "Sending his word and curing them, he snatched them from the Pit" (Ps. 107:20); "Down from the heavens, from the royal throne, leaped your all-powerful Word" (Wisd. of Sol. 18:15). Further, in the Tar-

gums—a post biblical collection of expanded translations of
the Old Testament—the Aramaic term *memra* often appears
as a synonym for the divine name of Yahweh and denotes the
presence of God. In the Targum of Gen. 3:8, for instance, it
is said that Adam and Eve "heard the sound of the Memra
walking in the garden." The significance of this usage comes
to light when we recall that the Aramaic *memra* corresponds
to the Hebrew *davhar,* meaning "word," which in turn is associated with the Greek *logos.* As we have seen, however,
there is a difference between the classical *logos* and the Hebrew *davhar,* which means both "word" and "thing" and may
be interpreted as action, event, or process.

Operating within this biblical and philosophical tradition,
Saint John takes the conceptual evolution of the logos a step
further. In the writings of Saint John the metaphor or the poetic
personification of the Word itself undergoes a metamorphosis;
the logos, or the Word, is rendered as a living entity, as spirit,
as a *who* and not a *what.* More than that, according to Saint
John, the Word is not only living but life itself (1 John 1:1),
and not one living thing has "its being but through him" (John
1:3). This last statement particularly reflects the influence of
the Hebrew notion of *davhar* on John's thinking. For the Hebrew mind (and Saint John was a Hebrew), the essential reality
of the *thing* was the *Word* of God. In his Gospel, Saint John
writes that in the synagogue at Capernaum, Jesus—the Word—
declared: "It is the spirit that gives life, the flesh has nothing
to offer. The words I have spoken to you are spirit and they
are life" (6:33). His Gospel also contains the teaching that
God is spirit (4:24), and in the Prologue we find the assertion
that God is the Word: "In the beginning was the Word: the
Word was with God and the Word was God" (1:1). Finally,
for the purpose at hand, Saint John's declaration that God is
love should be noted (1 John 4:8, 16).

The Johannine logos, therefore, may be defined as the
Word, God, spirit, and love. It is the house in which people
generate a living presence, the place where they are able to
dwell freely and openly (cf. John 8:32). It is the breath that
breathes life into the voice through which one speaks and by

which one is summoned. It is the call that comes from within and from beyond the human being. Regarded in such a manner, the Johannine logos bears certain implications for an approach to literature, the art whose vessel is made of language and whose vitality is born of the Word. Moreoever, unlike other art forms, literature requires its critic to respond in the medium of the art itself; one who answers the literary text must do so by summoning from himself a text of his own. Thus, quite apart from the complexities of theological considerations, the Johannine logos raises several issues pertaining to the study of literature and the response we bring to it. Specifically, Saint John's concept of the Word raises questions about the nature of literature, its relation to truth and reality, and the critical response it calls for.

Logos and Literature

Most literary theories approach literature with an eye toward its conformity to a given system or structure. The Freudians have their sexual coordinates, the Jungians their archetypes, and the Marxists their socioeconomic structure. The formalists and the structuralists also adhere to rigidly defined systems of poetics. Inasmuch as these theories are concerned with form, they are concerned with aesthetics, with *aisthetikos,* or perception. Similar to Edmund Husserl's conception of "the essence of phenomena," these theories of literature imply that the essence of literature "can be grasped and adequately determined in an immediate seeing." [1] The difference between William Shakespeare and Mickey Spillane, in this sense, lies in the beauty of the one over the baseness of the other, as anyone who has eyes can see. Literature, on this view, is material, an exalted form of mammon, made of little more than ink and paper. Instead of transforming matter into spirit, the aesthetic approach, at best, reduces spirit to matter. Thus what we are left with, in the words of Norman O. Brown, "is a materialization of the spirit; instead of the living spirit, the worship of a new material idol, the book." [2]

Approaching literature by the light of the living spirit, of the
Johannine logos, one discovers that literature has little to do
with aesthetics, where that term pertains to the appreciation of
beauty and form. The aesthetic outlook is enthralled by what
is pleasing to the eye; it is mesmerized by externals, such as
symmetry, pattern, and proportion, which, like the flesh, have
nothing to offer. The aesthetic endeavor is to prize the luster
of the letter rather than to respond to the call of the spirit; its
purpose is to calm rather than to disturb, to anesthetize rather
than to awaken. Appreciation leads us to settle into the comfort of complacent satisfaction, while awakening launches us
into critical collision: the living spirit lives in crisis, and the
presence of the individual is always in question. Lost in the
trappings of aesthetics, we lose our ability to declare, "Here I
am"; lulled by the splendor of the letter, the spirit sleeps the
sleep of Peter in Gethsemane. From the standpoint of the Johannine logos, literature calls forth passion, not appreciation;
it is a case of deep calling to deep, not of parade passing before
spectator. And the stake? Life itself.

Viewed as Word, as living spirit, literature is infinitely removed from the literalism of the letter, which commands the
movements of aesthetics: the literary is the opposite of the
literal, taken here to mean "of the letter." To paraphrase Paul,
the literal kills, while the literary gives life. Says Brown: "Literalism makes the world of abstract materialism, of dead matter. . . . Literalism kills everything. . . . Literalism makes a
universe of stone, and men astonished, petrified. Literalism is
the ministration of death, written and engraven in stone, tables
of stone and stony heart" (p. 223). The literary Word breathes
life into the soul; conceived as logos, the literary Word is precisely the life of the soul. The Word that vibrates in the breath
quickens the soul; the breath, the *pneuma,* that bears the intonations of the Word breathes living spirit into lifeless dust.
The function of the Word in literature, then, is not to imitate,
inform, entertain, or astonish but to summon its auditor to
life, just as Lazarus was summoned from the grave; it cries,
"Come forth!" Literature is marked not by its beauty but by

its beckoning; here lies the difference between Shakespeare and Spillane.

The structural, aesthetic approach to literature is characterized by diversion. It turns away from the open air of life toward the confines of the grave; its sytems offer the comforts of passivity and make for a sound sleep. Treated from the perspective of the Johannine logos, on the other hand, literature awakens us to confrontation. For as we are called, we are confronted, brought before the countenance. Once the eyes are free of the hypnotic influence of aesthetics, the ears may open up to literature's call. The call that rises up from literature confronts the reader with the same question that God put to Adam: "Where are you?" Listening for the logos in literature, one discovers that the reader's task is not the appreciation of beauty or form but the achievement of presence; and to be present, on the Johannine view, is to be present in relation to "the Word, who is life." Unlike schools of literary theory that regard literature as an It to be appreciated by a They, the notion set forth here is that literature is an I who addresses a Thou, that literature is spirit. It is not an object upon which I look but a living voice to which I respond, and the ability to respond is the ability to be present.

Literature is spirit, an I who addresses a Thou; or perhaps it is better to say that it dwells between an I and a Thou, enabling each to dwell. It may help to listen to Buber in this connection:

> In its human manifestation, spirit is a person's response to his Thou. . . . Spirit is word. . . . In truth, language is not situated in man, but rather man stands in language and speaks from it—so it is with all Word, with all spirit. Spirit is not in the I but between I and Thou. . . . Man lives in the spirit when he is able to respond to his Thou. It is the power of relation alone that enables man to live in the spirit.[3]

The "power of relation" that Buber mentions finds its highest expression in love. To the extent that a person lives in the spirit, he or she lives in love; to dwell is to live in love. Again, turning to Buber, we read, "Feelings abide in man, but man

dwells in his love" (p. 87). Conceived as love and applied to
literature, the Johannine logos suggests that literature itself is
conceived in love, in love's affirmation of love. If literature
arises between I and Thou to enable both to dwell, it is because
it enables both to love. The essence of literature? Love—love
of that which is all love.

Inasmuch as literature is instilled with love, it instills life
with love and, therefore, with meaning; for, like love of that
which is all love, meaning, in Buber's words, "is singly created out of the material of the element":

> *Meaning* is not, like the ark of those who protect themselves,
> constructed out of planks, with joints sealed up with pitch, but is
> singly created out of the material of the element, like the fiery
> chariot which carried Elijah away. One cannot scrape it together
> out of experience of just any kind nor does it let itself be taught
> and transmitted; rather it is joined to the soul as a primal posses-
> sion, to be unfolded and verified in its life-experience.[4]

Unfolded in life experience: "I am the life," says the logos
(John 14:6). If literature confronts us with the task of presence, it calls upon us to make it present in our life experience;
if literature is to transform our lives, we must transform it into
life. In this way literature "is joined to the soul" to give birth
to meaning, "created out of the material of the element," life
generated from life, logos born of logos. The literary gift to
life is life made literary and, therefore, meaningful.

If there should still be some confusion surrounding the relation between literature and life, it may be helpful to look to
a passage from *The Order of Things,* in which Foucault asserts
that literature

> breaks with the whole definition of *genres* as forms adapted to an
> order of representations, and becomes merely a manifestation of
> a language which has no other law than that of affirming—in op-
> position to all other forms of discourse—its own precipitous ex-
> istence; and so there is nothing for it to do but to curve back in a
> perpetual return upon itself, as if its discourse could have no other
> content than the expression of its own form; it addresses itself to
> itself as a writing subjectivity, or seeks to re-apprehend the es-

sence of all literature in the movement that brought it into being;
and thus all its threads converge upon the finest of points—
singular, instantaneous, and yet absolutely universal—upon the
simple act of writing.[5]

Foucault's remarks, to be sure, run counter to an aesthetic approach to literature, and the function of affirmation he refers
to might, at first glance, suggest something of love at work in
literature. But the affirmation Foucault invokes is a masturba-
tional self-affirmation; it is writing's embrace of itself rather
than the I's embrace of a Thou, literature's embrace of life.
The movement of literature is indeed a movement of return—the Word's return to the Word that was in the beginning,
"in the movement that brought it into being." But the I that
would "return upon itself" through literature must do so by
moving toward the Thou, and this it does by instilling its literature with love. In love lies the way to meaning.

Where there is meaning there is mean, a way; and where
there is a way, there is truth. "I am the Way and the Truth,"
says the logos (John 14:6). The presence achieved through the
response to literature's call is the presence of truth; only truth
can say, "Here I am." Thus "the truth consists not in knowing
the truth but in being the truth," as Søren Kierkegaard has
said,[6] and if literature is spirit, it is also truth.

Literature and Truth

Assuming that there is a relation between truth and reality, the
Johannine concept of the logos, or the Word, reveals something about the relation between literature and reality. On this
score there are at least two main currents of thought. First,
there is the idea that literature is a reflection of what reality is,
that literature is mimesis, to use the title of Erich Auerbach's
book. Reality is out there, and literature is the mirror held up
to it, revealing all that one loves and fears to behold. Whether
it reflects the shape of the subconscious, the superconscious,
or something in between, literature is but an image of the real.
The second general notion is that literature portrays not simply

what reality is but what it might or ought to become. In this instance literature has the propagandistic function of inspiring "a love of virtue and a horror of vice," as Denis Diderot puts it;[7] of course, what virtue and vice might entail depends on the propagandist. Nonetheless, whether it is regarded as a reflection of what reality is or as a hope for what it might become, literature is, in either case, viewed as something distinct from truth and reality. It informs by providing a formula, by declaring, "This is how it is" or "This is how it ought to be." In either case, imitation is the key.

According to the Johannine notion of the Word, however, both views of literature discussed above are wrongheaded. As for educational institutions where literature is presented in terms of imitation, Saint Augustine long ago uttered a warning applicable to them: "It is true that curtains are hung over the entrances to the schools where literature is taught, but they are not so much symbols in honor of mystery as veils concealing error."[8] And if it should be asked what the threat of the error is, we could turn to William Blake for an eloquent answer:

These are the destroyers of Jerusalem, these are the murderers
Of Jesus, who deny the Faith & mock at Eternal Life,
Who pretend to Poetry that they may destroy Imagination
By imitation of Nature's images drawn from Remembrance.[9]

Poetry is the opposite of the "imitation of Nature's images." Approached from the perspective of the Word, literature is not a lifeless object that reflects or projects reality; it is a living spirit engaged not in mimicry but in response, not in imitation but in evocation. Contrary to being distinct from life, truth, or meaning, as a mirror or a prescription is, literature is the very fabric of life, truth, and meaning.

Again, to view literature as spirit is to view it as truth, and truth cannot be imitated, dictated, or explicated. In the words of Brown, "Everything is told in parables. . . . The mystery of meaning remains forever inviolate; there is no literal truth" (p. 238). For meaning, says Brown, is "forever beyond the reach, the rape, of literal-minded explication; forever inviolate, forever new" (p. 264). Only the literal can imitate and be imitated, and regarding literature in terms of imitation is for the convenience of literal-minded explication, which is always rooted in formula. Once the truth is turned over to the stasis of a fixed formula, to the rigor mortis of the letter, it degenerates into a contented complacency that paralyzes the voice. We no longer speak but allow the formula in the mirror or in the mandate to speak for us. The letter kills by replacing the living Word with dead doctrine. No longer am I able to respond, "Here I am," but only "There it is, in black and white."

What, then, is literature's relation to truth and reality? According to Saint John, all that is, all that lives, has its being by virtue of the Word (see John 1:3). Taken as Word, literature does not mirror truth or reality but calls it forth, turning form into substance, matter into spirit. If the real is realization, as Jean-Paul Sartre has said,[10] so too is spirit. Truth, reality, meaning—they are always created, never discovered or imitated; literature, like the sculptor, does not release the form but hammers it out and breathes spirit into it. Truth lies in such a transformation; where there is no transformation there is no truth. Transformation is what lends literature its dimension of creativeness, and as Nicolas Berdyaev has pointed out, "true creativeness is always in the Holy Spirit, for only in the Spirit can there be that union of grace and freedom which we find in creativeness."[11] And what Berdyaev terms "Spirit," Saint John calls "logos." Only in the logos are we free to create, free to move; and literature is this movement.

Literature, then, is not an object but a process, forever in flux, dancing the dance of the Hindu god Shiva, creating and destroying with every step. Its epic heroes can shape nations; its human characters can change lives. In the light of this idea, it is easy to see why the effort to pin truth to the letter or to fix it in a formula is so tempting. If literature's relation to the truth is transformational, then I can never be sure of the ground beneath my feet; instead of rooting myself in firm ground, I must dance along the shifting edges of an abyss. Presence is always in question, and the certainty of the senses must be exchanged for the passion of faith, for the imagination of poetry. "Faith is the power of the imagination," writes Feuerbach, "which makes the real unreal and the unreal real: in direct contradiction with the truth of the senses, with the truth of reason." [12] In the fires of this imagination, literature and its truths are forged. William Blake, in "The Last Judgement," says, "This world of Imagination is the world of Eternity; it is the divine bosom into which we shall all go after the death of the Vegetated body" (p. 358).

The Johannine implications for the relation between literature and truth have been expressed to some extent in the annals of literary theory. In an echo of the assertion from John 1:3, Heidegger, for example, has said: "The being of all that is dwells in the Word. . . . Language is the house of being." [13] He has observed further that *Dichtung*—poetry or literature— "never draws on language as an existing raw material, but rather it is *Dichtung* itself that makes language possible." [14] The poet, in the words of Ralph Waldo Emerson, is the language maker,[15] and poetry is the truth maker, the vessel of the Word by which all that lives has its life. Literature is "the world of words which creates the world of things," to borrow a phrase of Lacan,[16] and not just things, but persons, ideas, and ideals are created by literature. If "song is existence," as Rilke has declared,[17] existence becomes what it is only in the singing. The world is not imitated by literature, but in literature it rises up and finds itself through the Word that was in the beginning. Literature is what makes the human being "capable of reuniting time and its source, and of giving back to God his own image." [18] We are capable of returning what we have been endowed with, because we have been endowed with language: man is the language of God, as a Hasidic master once said, and literature is the language of man. Says Wiesel: "Just Men compose the language with which God creates His universe. Prophets transmit the word of God, Just Men conceived it. Often in the form of tales." [19] And tellers of tales make storytellers of their listeners. In their words is couched the sum of a lifetime—and of the world. The world, therefore, is not the place of the Word; rather, the Word is the place of the world—and of life.

Only by regarding literature as life can truth be regarded as living spirit, as something that must be nurtured and cared for, something to hold dear. Indeed, Saint John suggests that holding truth dear is truth itself, that the logos is love of the logos, love of that which is all love. And what is said of the logos may be said of literature, if we associate literature with the Word. Here literature emerges not as an object of critical explication or appreciation but as a living subject to be loved; it is a passionate embrace, an affirmation, that calls for passionate embrace. The response it bids the reader to make, therefore, is always critical, both for the literature and for its respondent. This brings us to the third point in our examination of the Johannine logos and literary criticism, the critical response.

The Critical Response

To respond to a text in the light of the Johannine logos, the first thing a critic must do is divest himself or herself of all the cookbook methods of criticism that might predetermine a response to the literary text. If the critic fails to do this, then despite any experience or encounter with the text, a relation with the text cannot be established; and where the relation is lost, so is the truth. Rather than allow Marxism, structuralism, Freudianism, or any other -ism to speak for him, the critic must respond as he is beckoned. Again, the task with which literature confronts us is that of becoming present, and we become present through the voice, through the Word, by which we respond to the text. The text breathes into the critic the breath of life, and it is the critic's task to return what is given, for this is precisely how he receives the gift of life harbored in the Word.

The literary text is both a vehicle for and a response to the Word, which is the source of life; as such, it is a response that calls for a response. The study of literature is the study of the voice of existence, and as such it beckons the voice of personal existence, the voice of the critic. The word invoked in a literary text creates a structure of being by bringing into play the interrelations of the imaginary, the symbolic, and the real; indeed, this is just how parable works. A stage, a plot, or a moment is imagined and furnished with the symbols that call forth a living reality. A real King Lear, for example, is not required to get at the reality of Lear. Because the task of author and critic is accomplished through the Word, it is generated out of the division implied by the Word, the division of speaker and listener, of text and reader. The Word traces the "locus of difference," in Derrida's terms, which "marks the relationship with the other,"[20] thus making orientation possible. To be present is to be oriented in relation to something else, and the critic orients himself in relation to the text through an act of response: the voice of the critic brings him into relation with the voice of the poet. The process of reading the text, therefore, remains incomplete until the critic generates a text of his own—and it must be *his own*. This is how the critic becomes present before the text and before the Word, which rises up from the depths of the text.

Wherever the relation to the Word is an issue for critical response, presence is also an issue. But if the movement of reading and response revolves around a promulgation of presence, then it also turns on an implication of absence. First of all, as the voice of the text beckons me, I am drawn into the work, so that the act of reading removes me from my Here and projects me into the There, which constitutes the text as other. Moreover, I find my way there to the extent that I appropriate the voice that is there, making it part of my own voice. I read the paragraph, the stanza, the dialogue as the poet might read it, and the manner in which I read reflects the degree of my understanding. Yet I read only as the poet *might,* and my reading may reveal as much confusion as understanding. This is where absence makes itself felt: confused, disoriented, I am not quite sure where I stand in relation to the work. In my attempt to find my way there, I am, in the first instance, neither here nor there. The language of the text can thus become a veil that conceals the Word that it harbors; this is where my relation to the Word becomes critical.

This point of confusion and crisis is just what generates the need for understanding. The tension between presence and absence, the state of being in between, sets into motion the process of critical inquiry that distinguishes the critic as a living individual whose life is drawn from the Word. As Ortega y Gasset has observed, to feel oneself lost means, first of all, to feel oneself,[21] and sensing the absence of self before the Word in the literary text creates a situation in which the presence of self is called into question. Hence, in the words of Lacan, the void "is the first thing to make itself heard" (p. 248). The void is where the critic is asked, as Adam was asked, "Where are you?" Once the presence of self is called into question, critical response is called *for;* constituted by the Word and deriving its life from the Word, the self determines who it is by determining where it is. The process of response, then, traces the horizon of the critic's presence before the text, since, as Foucault states, "words have their *locus,* not in *time,* but in a *space* in which they are able to find their original site, change their positions, turn back upon themselves, and slowly unfold a whole developing curve: a *topological* space" (p. 114). Returning to her Here, the critic moves *at* the spot after having been removed *from* the spot.

At this point it is important to consider the elements of critical inquiry and response in more specific terms. The process of literary criticism may, in fact, be divided into three basic operations, which constitute a unified response to a text. The critic must first restate what the poet says, then reply to what the poet says, and, finally, communicate that reply to another by generating a text of his own.

By restating what the poet says, the critic enters into the discourse of another, a discourse into which a world is gathered. As he articulates the primary facets of the world view set forth by the poet, the critic brings into focus certain universals that find their expression in the particulars of the work at hand; Hamlet's question, Faust's desire, and Ivan Karamazov's burning indignation are a few familiar examples. Making the question, the desire, or the indignation his own, the critic encounters the eternal at work in the literary. This encounter makes the critic contemporary with the literature. The presence of the eternal in literature is what characterizes it as Word, in the Johannine sense of the term. In this vein, Paul Tillich has written, "There is no word from the Lord except the word which is spoken now." [22] The Word, the logos, which was spoken in the beginning is spoken now: before Abraham was, the logos is. The point in restating what the poet says is to lend an ear to the logos, to the Word that comes from the poet and from beyond him.

Having restated what the poet says, the critic next is summoned to reply, for the essence of the Word lies in the reply it evokes. This second step is not a separate operation; the critic does not respond after she has heard the Word, but rather her response is part of the hearing process. The critic's perception of the poet's world view remains incomplete until she adds her voice to the voice of the poet in such a way that the one is gauged by the other. Both are thus provided with definition and contour. As the critic measures the vision in her response alongside the vision to which she responds, she develops a faculty of hearing that transcends both. It is by virtue of hearing the other that the critic hears herself; her speaking, her response to the poet, is a hearing. She cannot hear the life-and-death question, "Where are you?" until she answers, "Here I am," and this response is precisely what tells her where she is.

Speaking implies the presence of someone spoken to; this is where the third phase of literary criticism comes in. To communicate to another—and to myself—my own position in relation to the poet's position, I must summon my reader in the same way that I have been summoned. That is, the Word I speak must call for a response; or better, it must call for a responsive hearing. Like the Johannine logos, the Word that calls for a responsive hearing bespeaks my being, my self, my presence or absence in relation to the Word. Moreover, just as I had assumed the position of another in articulating the poet's world view, I must now place myself in the position of another—my reader—in communicating my reply to the literary text. And how do I place myself in the position of another? By speaking lovingly and passionately in affirmation of the Word and the life it gives; otherwise, I am not present in the words I utter. Once again I arrive at my Here by way of a contextual There; to say, "Here I am," is to say, "That Thou art." Moving first in the direction of listener and then in the direction of speaker, I pass through myself in the capacity of both. Thus the final stage of criticism consummates the double movement of self-displacement, which calls my presence and my passion into question. Such is the movement at the spot that constitutes the self's becoming itself; and to become oneself is the project with which the Johannine logos confronts every person. Just as the work of art is the origin of the artist, so the critic's response is the origin of the critic.

By now one should have some sense of what the Johannine logos implies about the nature of literature, its relation to truth and reality, and the task it poses for the literary critic. The presence of the Word and the response that it calls for distinguish literature from other forms of writing; that is why a Dostoevsky beckons us so much more profoundly, more urgently, than a Harold Robbins. Just as the Voice called upon the prophet Isaiah to cry out (Isa. 40:6), so literature calls upon the critic. For the Word confronts and does not divert, making the critic's position critical indeed. The Word that resounds in literature underscores my need for redemption to the extent that I have not answered when I was called, that I have slept when I was asked to watch, that I have denied when I should have affirmed. When I thus engage in the critical task, my response to the voice that speaks takes on the nature of prayer; to be sure, the more my response is steeped in the living spirit of the Word, the more it assumes the aspects of prayer. The Thou whom we address when we speak the Word is the eternal Thou who addresses us. And, as Tillich has pointed out, "it is God Himself who prays through us, when we pray to Him. God Himself in us; that is what Spirit means. Spirit is another word for 'God present,' with shaking, inspiring, transforming power" (p. 137). If the critic is shaken, transformed, then he knows he has responded to the one who speaks.

Who, then, speaks? Foucault tells us that when Friedrich Nietzsche asked this question, Stéphane Mallarmé replied, "The being of the Word itself" (p. 305). If one should add to this "the being of the Word who is God," one must bear in mind what Buber points out when he, too, asks, "Who speaks?" He declares that

> It would be of no use to us to reply with the word "God," if we do not do so out of that decisive hour of personal existence when we had to forget everything we imagined we knew of God, when we dared to keep nothing of the conventional, nothing learned or self-contrived, no shred of knowledge, and were plunged into the Night.[23]

Only when we have reached this depth can we plumb the depths of the living Word that is present in literature; only then can we enter into the play of deep calling to deep; only then can we move over the face of the deep, as did the logos that was in the beginning.

CHAPTER THREE

Lacan's *Parole* and the Literary Critic

I HAVE EXAMINED the implications of the Johannine logos for the process of literary criticism and the critic's task of generating presence through the Word. It has also been pointed out that Saint John's concept of the logos, or the Word, is not a religious aberration but has Greek and Judaic contexts. To determine whether another thinker from another time might bear similar implications for the literary critic, let us now consider Jacques Lacan's notion of the *parole,* or the Word, and the light that it may shed on the critical endeavor. This examination will show that the perspectives on literary criticism taken from the Johannine Word are not peculiar to a single tradition or discipline but emerge from a much larger scope of concern.

Lacan has been described as the curious product of Georg Wilhelm Hegel, Sigmund Freud, and Martin Heidegger. He associates himself with the Freudian school of psychoanalysis and has had such thinkers as Jacques Derrida in his seminars. The question of how the self shapes and relates to itself is one of his central concerns, and he is interested in the structure of the self within the structural context of language. Frederick Jameson has correclty pointed out that Lacan's *The Language of the Self* is "the best introduction to Lacan in English," [1] for it contains not only a representative work by Lacan but a helpful and detailed commentary by Anthony Wilden.

The essay that appears in *The Language of the Self* originally was published in the first volume of *La psychanalyse*

(1956) under the title "Fonction et champ de la parole et du langage en psychanalyse" and was later included in Lacan's *Écrits* (1966). Although in the essay Lacan makes no explicit reference to the literary critic, his thoughts on how the self gives voice to its subjective existence carry implicit ramifications for what happens to the critic in formulating a reply to a literary text. The psychoanalytic subject, for example, faces the task of unearthing some truth about himself and about the world within the context of a discourse, that is, through a process of hearing and speaking; his task, in other words, is to know himself, to create a presence of self, through the act of response. This chapter shows that the problem the psychoanalytic subject confronts in generating a language of the self is like the difficulty the literary critic faces in generating a response to a text.

I have divided my remarks on Lacan's "Fonction" and the literary critic into three sections: (1) the Word (Lacan's *parole*) as the language of the self; (2) the Otherness of the critic and the otherness of the text; and (3) the truth born in the Word. For the Word, the self, the Other, and the truth are the terms that provide the keys for unlocking the relation between Lacan's *parole* and the literary critic.

The Word as the Language of the Self

To make sense of a language of the self, one must first distinguish between a language that is peculiar to the self and the language of the world at large, the language of what Heidegger calls *Das Man*," or "the They." [2] The language of *Das Man* has a strictly external orientation; it is grounded in the network of the crowd, where inner subjectivity—the sense of soul or self—is deemed either illusory or irrelevant. Personal "reality" is rooted in one's slot within the coordinate system that comprises the world; we see as the world sees and speak as it demands: I am a teacher, a husband, a father, a Democrat, a jogger, an American, and so on. The language of *Das Man* provides us with a *Man-selbst*, or "They-self," contoured to comfortably situate itself, and thereby lose itself, in the crowd.

It is the language of positioning, defining the *what* of a fixed identity and pointing the way to the next step along a predetermined path. Instead of living in the spirit of decisiveness, the individual allows the event to decide for her. Staking out the signposts of direction, the language of *Das Man* is not the language by which we speak but by which we are spoken; it is the language that insists on unity and ubiquity. And, as Lacan points out, to the extent that the individual is thus locked into the "stereotypes of discourse," the Word is absent and the self lost.[3] For within the stereotypes of a discourse, I allow the appropriate phrase in a given language game to speak for me rather than speak any response of my own. I imprison myself in a liturgy that is proper to my labels and titles; thus confined, the self is unable to breathe, unable to move, unable to become itself—in short, it is no self.

"I identify myself in language," Lacan asserts, "but only by losing myself like an object" (pp. 299–300). Establishing an identity through the language of *Das Man* reduces the individual to an objectlike status, because it reduces him to an objectlike stasis. The dynamic of existing, the process of becoming, is suspended in the attempt to take one's bearings; the subject situates himself by getting hold of himself, bringing himself to a halt. Whenever I identify myself in language I bring myself to a public setting, where I take note of my nakedness and clothe myself in shame. Here, again, personal "reality" is strictly external, like that of an object, and personal presence is determined within the context of a network of established signifiers. The subjective division between the "am" and the "am-not-yet," which sets the subject in motion, arises only when an inward dialogue begins to interfere with the outward chorus, and this is where the Word emerges as the language of the self, a language that summons the self to being. Because the Word comes forth in dialogue, one way to make a distinction between the Word and the language of the crowd is to say, as Lacan does (pp. 247, 298) that every Word calls for a response. To be sure, this is what it means to be summoned. Moreover, wherever the language of the self is an issue, the individual's responding is a hearing, and this introduces the added dimension that creates the dialogue of inward-ness. The announcement of identity, on the other hand, brings the individual to a stop and seeks no reply, no movement; it seeks only to situate through appellation and assignment.

In his commentary contained in *The Language of the Self,* Anthony Wilden explains that, like Heidegger, "Lacan views the subject as subordinated to language and thus cuts across the distinction often made between interpersonal and intraper-sonal relations by representing the second as a subset of the first in the chain of signifiers which link them." [4] But to claim that Lacan takes intrapersonal relations to be a subset of inter-personal relations may be rather misleading, if that is assumed to mean the one is somehow less than the other. Perhaps it would be more accurate to say that the intrapersonal relation is made possible only in the light of the interpersonal relation; that is, the individual determines her presence or subjectively approaches herself only by way of another subject. As Wiesel says, Adam's first question was not "Who am I?" but "Who are you?" [5]

Only the self, whose language is the Word,can make such a determination of self; only the self can ask, "Who?" Here we discover the distance and the difference between living subject and the anonymous crowd, which can only ask, "What?" But because the subject develops a sense of himself by way of the crowd, his relation to himself is reflected in his relation to those around him. The soul suffers what it inflicts. All external division has an internal analogue, an inner rift that is mediated by establishing a dialogical link between the individual and the community. The following remarks from Jameson may help in this regard:

> We are thus entitled to speak of an insertion of the subject here, both in the relationship of the historical figure to his sit-uation and in the project of the psychobiography as a recon-struction of it: the opposition of particular to universal has been transformed into the relationship of an impersonal and rigorously interchangeable consciousness to a unique historical configura-tion. This said, it must also be noted that the psychobiographical

form remains shackled to the categories of individual experience, and is thus unable to reach a level of cultural and social generalization without passing through the individual case history. [Pp. 343–44]

But since individual case history is always incomplete—at least until death—passing through it is a continual process. The consciousness of soul and the presence of self must forever be regenerated and are continually in question. Though the task has been met a million times, it always remains to be done. The ultimate constitutive Word of and about the self is forever yet to be uttered. Thus we are reminded of Bakhtin's assertion that "the definition given to me lies not in the categories of temporal being but in the categories of the *not-yet-existing*."[6] Where there is presence, there is interplay with absence.

Since the project of forging itself is constantly yet to be completed, the self dwells along the edges of a kind of fragmentation or within the division implied by incompletion. Hence critics such as Robert Con Davis assert, "The Lacanian subject is a subject alive and in motion that can never be known directly, but can be known only in its absence, in the traces it leaves behind: in the presence of an absence that is language."[7] As the language of the self, the Word implies division. Or better: the Word implies a dialectical process of creating and closing division. While the language of the crowd is geared to unity through conformity and would have the last word, the Word calls for response and responds to the call. The self *is* the calling and responding; it *is* the process of speaking and hearing and speaking again. The Word is the language of process. The Word is the language of the spirit.

"The spirit," says Lacan, "is always somewhere else" (p. 270). In psychoanalytic terms, neurosis is the result of a paralysis of voice that brings the individual to a standstill when she cannot move beyond the nothingness of what she is *not yet;* it occurs when the flux of discourse is arrested and the subject is frustrated by the impotence to speak what she longs

to become. The self is posited, then, on the basis of a spiritual
loss or a discovery of difference, yet the difficulty for the subject is to sustain a separate autonomy without being swallowed
up by the nothingness of the *not*. This is where the motion or
the process engendered by the Word comes in: the first thing
to make itself heard is the silence of the void, and this is what
sets up the dialectic of the spirit. Lacan explains:

> It was indeed the *verbe* that was in the beginning, and we live in
> its creation, but it is the action of our spirit that continues this
> creation by constantly renewing it. And we can come back to this
> action only to the extent that we allow ourselves to be constantly
> pushed ahead by it. [P. 271]

Coming back to the creative act initiated by the *verbe* that was
in the beginning: the movement forward is a movement of return. But the movement does not lie in being "pushed ahead,"
as Lacan suggests; the movement comes in a leap by which we
free ourselves from the anesthetizing hold of *Das Man*.

The language of *Das Man* sets up a restraining net of categories or signifiers, while the Word sets up a motion. The language of *Das man* seeks the objective code of necessity, while
the Word seeks the voice of possibility for the subjective existence of the self. The relation between the language of *Das
Man* and the Word is not one of set versus subset but one
of set versus counterset. This is why, in explaining Lacan,
Wilden writes,

> For the complete message of the conscious subject to be under-
> stood (by the emitter or by the receiver) at any level at all, there
> must be an unconscious reading in reverse at the *end* of the mes-
> sage, a reference to the locus of the code *after* the complete mes-
> sage has been received. [P. 275]

The reversed reading is the counter to the set that constitutes the
"locus of the code," and the reversal of the reading marks
the passage through personal case history, which, in turn, allows for the *nonfunctional* insertion of the subject. That is, the
Word places the subject at the scene without turning him over
to a market of exchange.

This brings us to another distinction that Lacan makes between language and the Word: "To the extent that language becomes more functional, it is rendered improper for the Word; and as it becomes too particular to us, it loses its function as language" (pp. 298–99). So now we have the language of *Das Man* as that which calls for no response and is functional; and we have the Word as that which calls for a response and is nonfunctional. But if, as implied in the preceding paragraph, the language of *Das Man* situates the individual within a market of exchange, the two preceding distinctions may create confusion. After all, doesn't the language of negotiation call for a response, and isn't it functional? One may reply to such an objection, however, by pointing out that the language of negotiation calls for a response precisely for the purpose of putting an end to response, for a *settlement;* the Word calls for response for the sake of response, for a *repetition.* The discourse of exchange always has an end in view, while the call of the Word is, for all "practical" purposes, pointless. Thus as the self becomes increasingly a substantial self, it becomes increasingly groundless; as the subject moves toward himself, he edges toward the abyss. And because such an individual has been shaped by the voice of the crowd, by the text of the other, the so-called authentic self arises as the outstanding text of a self that is the Other.

The Otherness of the Critic and the otherness of the Text

Perhaps it is best to begin this section with Lacan's fundamental, simplified Schema L, which represents what Lacan regards as a topology of the self (see fig. 1; cf. Lacan, p. 53). As Wilden explains the figure, the *S* (Es) represents the subject's ineffable and stupid existence; the *a* (other) his objects; the *á* (*moi*) what is reflected of his form in his objects; and the *A* (Other) the locus from which the question of his existence may be put to him (pp. 107–108). To this it may be helpful to add Jameson's explanation:

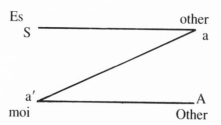

Figure 1. Lacan's simplified Schema L (based on a diagram by Lacan in *The Language of the Self*, p. 53).

The subject's conscious desire, which he understands as a relationship between the desired object (a) and his ego or self (á), is mediated by the more fundamental relationship between the real subject (S) and the capital A of the Other, language or the Unconscious. In the dynamic version of this topology . . . this structure of the subject is as it were put in motion by the movement of desire, considered as a *parole* or act of enunciation. [P. 366]

Once more: the *S* is the individual's physical presence, his flesh and blood; the *a* is the thing that interests him, that commands his attention; the *á* is the part of him that is interested, his attentive consciousness; and the *A* is the part of him that is yet to be, which summons him by questioning him.

The *parole,* the Word, constitutes the question—or rather calls into question—and sets the individual in motion. "What I seek in the Word," Lacan writes, "is the response of the other. What constitutes me as subject is my question" (p. 299). The critical inquiry, the question, is an indicator of division, and the critic seeks a response from the text—the resonance of the Word—which may close the division. From a Lacanian point of view, the division or distance between the critic and the text reflects an inner division within the critic herself. The question, "What is this text about?" harbors another question: "What am I about?" As Wilden observes, for Lacan, language is a movement toward something, "as dependent upon the notion of *lack* as is the theory of desire" (p. 164); and the thing which the self lacks is precisely itself. The inquiry concerning the text, then, is an inquiry concerning the self, an effort to move toward the "authentic" or "unrealized" self posited as the Other. And it is the Word, the *parole*, that launches the self into this movement over the face of its own void.

The manner in which the text speaks to me is determined by the manner of my questioning, which is itself a kind of text. And since my question is, "What constitutes me as subject?" I am structured like a text, like language. Thus Lacan asserts:

> The form in which language is expressed defines subjectivity. Language says, "You will go this way, and when you see that, you will turn there." To put it differently, language refers itself to the discourse of the other [in this case the text]. It is enveloped as such within the highest function of the Word, insofar as the Word engages its author by investing the one to whom it is spoken with a new reality. [P. 298]

Wiesel has written that hearing a tale can alter the tale itself.[8] But the tale is altered only to the extent that its listener is altered. Indeed, as Ellie Ragland-Sullivan has noted, "within a Lacanian worldview, there can be no rational, classical, objective reader who approaches a text which is a discrete, contained, and separate entity, for each was structured by the language surrounding it and each will operate its own linguistic possibilities on the other in an intersubjective dialectic."[9] When the Word envelops the critic's response to a literary text, the text is invested with a new reality. Calling forth a new reality is the function of the Word, as it is released from the stereotypes of a standing discourse. And, in the language of Lacan, the reality that is yet to be is the Other, "the locus of human intellect and the ground of human becoming," as Stuart Schneiderman describes it.[10]

Preceding the new reality, however, is an imaginary relation at work in the critic's approach to the text. Taking Lacan's terminology a bit further, when the critic comes to a text, he takes up an imaginary relation that links him to the text qua *moi;* indeed, the *moi* is shaped by the relation, since the *moi,*

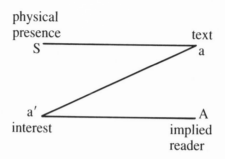

Figure 2. Lacan's Schema L adapted to the critical process.

or the interested I, is molded by its interest in the text. Regarding the critic who subscribes, for example, to a Freudian
school of thought, the imaginary relation is grounded in
Freudianism. As the critic addresses the text and listens for its
reply, the spirit or truth of the process is judged from a third
position, from the position of the Other. In this case the Other
might be described as the critic's implied reader; and because
it is the *critic's* implied reader, the relation between the *moi*
and the Other provides the scene for the critic's Word, which
is the language of the critic's self. As a judge, the Other determines the authenticity of the critic, the critic's truth. John
Brenkman states this idea in his piece on Lacan by saying,
"The existence of the Other guarantees the truth of the philosophical [critical] discourse, and the Other's own self-identity,
or presence, guarantees the philosopher's [critic's] eventual
identity with it." [11] The testimony to be imparted to the implied
reader must be embraced first of all by the critic; he must become the truth he struggles to voice. This means that the critic
is faced with a process of self-analysis, and the appeal to the
Other is what makes his self-analysis possible.

At this point it is helpful to introduce the simplified Schema
L as it applies to the process of critical inquiry (see fig. 2).
Comparing figure 2 with figure 1, we see that in figure 2 the *S*

corresponds to the person who sits in her study and labors over the quaint and curious volume. Opposite the critic is the *a,* the black and white of the literary text which commands the critic's conscious interest; the *a* is the critic's "desired object," as Jameson calls it, because it is the thing she longs to grasp, to comprehend. "The text has for us authority," Shoshana Felman points out, "the very type of authority by which Jacques Lacan defines the role of the psychoanalyst in the structure of transference." [12] The desired object in turn, is linked to the critic's interested ego, or the *á,* which seeks some understanding of itself through its understanding of the text. Finally, the capital *A,* the Other, is the implied reader, who, like the Other, "is unreal, but not imaginary" (Schneiderman, p. 30). This is the one to whom the critic responds through her response to the text; it is for the sake of the Other, with whom she longs for a relation, that she seeks the truth born in the Word.

Jane Gallop's reading of Lacan in her book *Reading Lacan* bears some different implications which should be addressed at this point. She is quite correct in suggesting that when Lacan's ideas are applied to the literary critic, "the critic is no longer analyst but patient"; [13] however, she misplaces the Other in the schema of critical response when she asserts that

> the desire to know what the Other knows, so as to know what one desires so as to satisfy that desire, is the drive behind all quests for knowledge. . . . We read to learn what the Other (what the Author) knows, to learn what are his desires, in the hope of understanding and satisfying our own. [P. 185]

The implied reader—l'Autre—is not the Author but is rather situated in a third position, in the position of truth. In a sense, the implied reader to whom the critic must respond is the word from which the text is born and in which the truth is born. Indeed, it will be recalled that Lacan himself identifies the Other as the one in a third position, which is the realm of truth (see Wilden, p. 269). Gallop does not address the issue of the implied reader; for her, the implied reader is Lacan, the Dead Author, for whom she longs and from whom, in a dream, she gains approval (p. 187). Desiring to know what Lacan knows, she proceeds as if Lacan knew all, as if Lacan were himself the truth. Thus she engages in the ultimate act of transference, replacing the Other with the Author—Lacan—and losing both. In doing so, moreover, she loses the relation to the truth in which her presence as critic is grounded.

Schneiderman argues that the problem "posed by the Other as the place of language undercuts the metaphysics of presence" (p. 29). Whether or not this is the case, it does not undercut the *issue* of the critic's presence, for what is at stake in the critical process is the existence of the critic himself. Because the discovery of self is the discovery of loss, the self presents itself as a task, as something that must be created through the Word. So considered, the critical endeavor is essentially *poetic,* in the sense of the Greek *poiein,* which means "to bring into being." Like the artist and his work, the dancer and the dance, the critic and his activity are of a piece; just as the poem is the origin of the poet, the critical response is the origin of the critic. He creates himself by drawing his relationship to the text into the relationship of himself as *moi* to himself as Other, as his own implied reader. The implied reader, it should be noted, is not generated by the question of what They want to hear but by the problem of what the critic must speak and how he gives voice to himself. On such a view, the critic does not pick up a text by Johann von Goethe, Fyodor Dostoevsky, or James Joyce simply to communicate some new observations on the literature; nor does he set his pen to paper to contribute to the hallowed corpus of Human Knowledge, though this may well be what he claims he is doing. There is no casually coming across the outcry of a Faust, a Karamazov, or a Daedalus, no munching on buttery popcorn as we move through those paragraphs. Here the critic encounters only critical collision, a collision that brings him face to face with a Kierkegaardian either/or: either flight or resolve.

Resolve is always resolve for the truth or a "truthful structure," to use Lacan's term. Felman has observed that such a structure is generated through "openness to a linguistic passage through the Other," through "*resonating in the Other,*" through the "capacity for *passing through the Other.*" [14] This resonance and passage are represented both in Lacan's Schema L (figure 1) and in my own modification of it (figure 2). Wilden characterizes it as "an initial and a later relationship, as well as a dynamic process" (p. 162). Although the line that links the reference points in the schema remains unbroken, it is forever in flux. Moreover, the thing that makes the process dynamic also makes it dialectical, as Lacan suggests:

> For in this labor through which the subject endeavors to reconstruct a construct *for an other*, he discovers again the fundamental alienation which made him construct it *like an other*, and which has always destined it to be stripped from him *by an other*. [P. 249]

Linking Lacan's statement to my modification of his Schema L, we see that the critic constructs her criticism *for* the text and *as* her implied reader in a movement toward her Other. But to the extent that she has embraced the Word in her undertaking, her critical inquiry seeks the response of the Other, a response that is itself an inquiry, calling the whole process into question; as such, the inquiry strips the critic of her finished construct. Thus the process must be repeated; having signed her name to her tract, the critic must descend again into the inner dimension of the literary text and listen for the summons of the Word.

The limit of this repetition? Death. Lacan writes:

> The limit drawn by death is at every instant present in what history contains as achieved. It represents the past under its real form; that is, not the physical past, the existence of which is abolished, nor the epic past, since it is perfected by memory, nor the historical past, where man finds the guarantor of his future. Rather, the past under its real form is that which manifests itself as reversed in repetition. [P. 318]

In other words, death is present in the critical process as the only authentic end to the process, so that the reality of the process lies in the will to repetition, even unto death. The situation, however, is not as dark as it may seem at first glance. For it is the project embraced even unto death that robs death of its sting. Such a project must be fueled by a passion and a love that eclipse the monolith of death. The resolve for repetition, the decision to return, is steeped in the critic's ability to love his reader as he loves himself and to love the Word with all his heart and soul. In this way his life is given rather than stolen; in this way he gains his life by losing it.

Hence the Word, which structures the Otherness of the critic and the otherness of the text, finds its voice among the shadows of death cast by the flames of life. The Word is the language of the self; the self is at stake in the critical inquiry; and death is the horizon for the process of repetition that sustains the self. It must also be pointed out that death is not regarded here as "the end," but as what Heidegger calls "a way of being-toward-the-end" (p. 245). Death does not befall us, as the crowd, referring to the obituaries, would hae us believe. Death is a way of being characterized by a movement forward, downward, and upward, a movement toward the truth. The critic's endeavor is an occasion for a last judgment, where the truth of the critic's existence is called into question. The Word calls; and through response, truth is born in the Word.

Truth Born in the Word

Through response, the birth of truth: through the Word, the revelation. Truth is a living thing, something born. It comes not at the end of syllogistic speculation but in revelation, when we have divested ourselves of the axioms and -isms that eclipse the Word and conceal the deed. Once again, let us see what Lacan has to say:

> The hysterical revelation of the past . . . is not so much a matter of falsehood. Rather, the revelation presents us with the birth of truth in the Word and thus confronts us with the reality of what is neither true nor false. . . . For the truth of the revelation lies in the present Word which bears witness to it in the reality at hand and which grounds it in the name of that reality. Indeed, within this reality the Word alone testifies to that element of the powers of the past that has been cast aside at every crossroad where the event has made the decision. [Pp. 255–56]

Not only is the Word born through revelation—the Word itself is revelation, its source and substance. The "hysterical revelation of the past . . . presents us with the birth of truth in the Word," because the past is made present or presented to us through the Word. For the critic, the revelation of the past means the revelation of the method's threat to selfhood.

At this point it is important to distinguish between having lived and having a past. Those who somnambulistically plod through the crowd and its recitations have no past. The individual, on the other hand, comes into possession of a past by recognizing or *owning* what was done and the spirit in which it was done. In her article "Beyond Oedipus," Felman notes that, for Lacan, recognition is "essentially a speech-act, whose symbolic action *modifies* the subject's history, rather than cerebrally observing or recording it" (p. 1026). As a speech-act or an act of the Word, Felman goes on to explain, such recognition entails "the acknowledgement of responsibility for the discourse of the Other in oneself" (p. 1027). In Heidegger's words, this is how "genuine historicity" weans us "from the conventions of *Das Man*" (p. 391). A person owns her past by speaking it, by responding to it, thus becoming response-able, capable of answering for himself. Truth in this case denotes not something known but a way of existing, and its opposite is the Sartrian *mauvaise foi*—bad faith—or the Heideggerian veiling of the Open, as Jameson has suggested (p. 383). The truth does not conceal but reveals; its essence lies not in its conformity to fact but in its ability to rend the shrouds that we draw over ourselves. The Word finds its presence, then, not so much in the content of a response as in what is happening to me when I am making a response. Truth born in the Word is truth as subjectivity.

This brings us to a distinction between objective and subjective thought, which parallels the distinction between the language of the They and the Word as the language of the self. Kierkegaard's explanation of the difference between the two is a helpful one:

> While objective thought is indifferent to the thinking subject and his existence, the subjective thinker is, as an existing individual, essentially interested in his own thinking, existing as he does in his thought. . . . While objective thought translates everything into results and helps all mankind to cheat by copying these off and reciting them by rote, subjective thought puts everything into process and omits the result.[15]

Again, truth cannot be chiseled into a formula. Truth born in the Word is conceived in a state of dance, suspended over the abyss by the passion of the self. Just as the living individual is in process, so is the truth; indeed, the truth *is* the process through which the living person generates her presence. And the progenitor of the process? The Word.

Truth is subjectivity. Truth is born in the Word. The Word is the language of the self. These statements lead us to a metaphysics of speaking which suggests, with Kierkegaard, that "the crowd is untruth," [16] for the language of the crowd is the language of *Das Man,* the language of the school of thought, the opposite of the Word. We have seen that the Word implies both the separation and the union of listener and speaker, both within and around the self. It creates and closes the gaps of sound and silence, of presence and absence. As soon as we speak the metaphor and thus cast our net over the truth, the distance reappears and beckons. There is no fixed truth waiting to be snared; there is only the struggle to voice it. Or better: the struggle is itself the truth, and the self is the struggle it engages in. Truth is subjectivity.

From Lacan's standpoint, regarding the truth as subjectivity means that to be an authentic self is to have a decisive past, a past that has been willed and not left to the event or to the prescriptions of the critical method. Authenticity means presence, and the presence or absence of the self turns on the presence or absence of a language of the self. Wherever the self is present, truth is born in the Word.

But what, exactly, does this business about truth born in the Word mean to the literary critic? First of all, it frees him from a past that has been patterned by knowledge or by a given critical -ism. T. S. Eliot may help in this regard:

> The knowledge imposes a pattern, and falsifies,
> For the pattern is new in every moment
> And every moment is a new and shocking
> Valuation of all we have been.[17]

Instead of mechanically following the pattern that has been determined in the past, the critic must seek the truth through the revelation that launches him ahead in the process of becoming something other, something more, than what he is. And because truth born in the Word is truth as subjectivity, the critic must lend an ear to the Teacher within if the revelation is to open up to him. Insofar as the critic's relation to his activity is an index of his relation to himself, the critic *is* the relation. His relation to himself is his relation to what he is by virtue of what he has been. Since the critical inquiry says something about the critic's past (and here lies the "shocking valuation"), the manner in which he responds to the text reveals something about his ability to respond to his past. And since his response is undertaken for the sake of his Other—that is, for the sake of the self which he is *not yet*—the critical inquiry reveals something about the critic's process of becoming. Wilden goes so far as to identify the subject or the critic with this opposition of presence and absence (p. 191); similarly, Schneiderman asserts that the presence or absence of the self turns on the presence or absence of language, an opposition that is set up by the discourse of inquiry (p. 30).

The truth of the critic's presence, then, rests on this response-ability. The critic who turns to a Freudian, Marxist, or structuralist formula owns no past, establishes no presence, and speaks no truth. It is the -ism, not the critic, that makes the response, which, indeed, is more a recitation than a response. In such an instance the critic is not a speaking self but a self spoken by the formula, that is, no self. She engages in no struggle to voice a language of the self; instead, to borrow a phrase from Lacan, she attempts a "seduction of the other by the means with which he complies and through which he constructs the monument of his narcissism" (p. 248). There is no Other for whom she speaks, since there is nothing that she is in the process of becoming. And so she is herself nothing, seeking only the reinforcement of playback from her audience, only the mirror image of herself, which she takes to be proof of her personal presence. Further, as if the joke were not cruel enough, the mirror image is not an echo of the critic's self but merely a reflection of what the -ism has made her. Hence the Word is absent, the critic lost, and the truth aborted: the only thing left is the fixed and ready reaction of the code that would have the last word.

It is easy enough to see why the comfort and complacency of the code might be preferable to the fear and trembling of hysterical revelation. Because the critic has at stake his subjective existence as determined by his response capability and his responsibility for that existence, he comes before a judgement. In this connection Lacan speaks of "attaining a subjective realization of being-for-death" (p. 279). As indicated above, when the critic establishes a relation to his past through a response, he gives his past a presence. Likewise, he instills his future anterior with a presence and thus makes himself contemporary with his death. Through his Other, the critic is judged according to the depth of his resolve to become what he is *not yet,* that is, according to his being-for-death; he is judged, in other words, on the basis of his relation to the truth born in his Word. The critic's relation to death is also a reflection of his power of self-creation, since the creative process of coming to be entails a destructive process of dying away. To the extent that the critic speaks and does not mimic, his speaking or inquiry changes him; this too is what the Other judges him for—how much and how deeply he has changed. The real import of a given piece of literary criticism thus lies not so much in what it says as in the kind of silence it leaves within the critic. Here, in silence, the truth is most itself, for the silence generates the ensuing response to the Word. Silence judges.

We may now have a better idea of what is meant by "truth born in the Word." The birth of truth is the birth of presence for the critic, a rebirth that occurs in the reaffirmation of dialogical presence out of ontological absence, a return whose needfulness announces itself in every undermining of the self. Truth does not console or reassure; no, it disturbs, even destroys, the stasis of narcissism. Giving birth to truth means rising from the ashes of crisis, and this makes the critic's undertaking critical in every sense of the word. For giving birth to truth means giving death to a counterfeit self by revealing a "lie" or prior condition of bad faith. It means turning away from the deceptive reinforcement of the mirror and venturing forth without the preoccupation with how I look or sound. It means hammering out a presence of self by undoing all support of self.

Conclusion

If a method can be derived from the foregoing considerations, it would perhaps be best to structure it along the lines of pertinent questions rather than ready answers. First, the movement toward the Word as the language of the self begins by asking, "How am I speaking?" That is, am I parroting a formal body of discourse, or am I bringing to the scene my own literary dimension? Next, the Otherness of the critic and the otherness of the text are approached by asking, "For whom am I speaking?" That is, am I chattering at the image of myself in the mirror, mouthing what the crowd wants to hear; or is my speaking a hearing, a struggle to find the voice of the Other who I am not yet? Finally, the birth of the truth in the Word is initiated by asking, "Why am I speaking?" That is, am I speaking to buttress a given construct, to tighten my grip on my handrails, or am I speaking for the sake of encounter and judgment? And addressing all of these questions entails the response to the one critical question the critic is summoned to answer: "Where are you?" Looking for existing examples of such a "method," Kierkegaard's observations on Shakespeare and Goethe,[18] Lev Shestov's treatment of Dostoevsky,[19] and Albert Camus's remarks on Franz Kafka immediately come to mind.[20]

I have proposed in this chapter that the existence of the individual critic is at stake in the critical process, and that this
problem is precisely what has been ignored by the various
schools of literary criticism. When asked why we bother to
read and criticize literature, one may respond in various ways:
we read and criticize literature to learn more about a given
body of literature, to discover something about the political
and social progression of historical materialism, to sharpen
our aesthetic sensitivity, to find out something about human
beings' psychological makeup, to approach an understanding
of the nature of human beings, to add publications to our ten-
ure files, and so on. But, again, it must be asked, what is the
interest in all this, what does all this *matter* to the individual
who has to carry on with the business of living? And the only
way to sustain this question is to avoid the formula, the fixed
expression that characterizes the ongoing cookbook methods
of criticism, the methods by which the self becomes trapped
into being a spoken self, no self.

In the language of Lacan, the cookbook approach must be
ultimately "resolved, dissolved, and absolved" through the
"exegesis, invocation, and dialectic" of the critic:

> Hieroglyphics of hysteria, blazons of phobia, labyrinths of the
> *Zwangsneurose*—charms of impotence, enigmas of inhibition,
> oracles, of dread—talking arms of character, seals of self-
> punishment, disguises of perversion—such are the hermetisms
> that our exegesis resolves, the equivocations that our invocation
> dissolves, the artifices that our dialectic absolves, in a deliverance
> of the imprisoned sense, which moves from the revelation of the
> palimpsest to the given word [*mot*] of mystery and to the pardon
> of the Word. [P. 281]

The pardon of the Word: this last phrase points up the need for
one last observation on Lacan's *parole* and the literary critic.
It tells us that instead of being the one who knows, the critic
is the one in error; he is the one who must overcome what he
knows in order to become what he is. If he is to get at the truth
about a text, he must unearth the truth about himself; his task
is not so much to inform another as to increase himself through

his embrace of another in the Word. In this way, the Word absolves him and thus frees him of the phobia and the dread, of the impotence and the perversion, through which he has lost himself in the language of *Das Man*. Thus pardoned and liberated, he can say at last, "Here I am."

CHAPTER FOUR

Dostoevsky's *Dvoinik* per Lacan's *Parole*

HAVING EXAMINED THE IMPLICATIONS of Lacan's *parole* for the literary critic, let us consider its implications for the critical approach to a specific literary text. As such an investigation, this chapter provides an example of a response to a literary work in which personal presence achieved through the Word is an issue in the work itself. The chapter demonstrates that Lacan's concept of the Word is applicable not only to the literary critic but to the literary character and the relationships that define him. For this purpose I have selected Dostoevsky's *Dvoinik*, or *The Double* (1846),[1] a novel in which the difficulty confronting the main character is fundamentally the same as the difficulty confronting the critic.

There have been numerous studies of *Dvoinik*, but all have failed to examine the structure of self represented by the protagonist, Golyadkin, as a structure of language. Dostoevsky's elder contemporary V. G. Belinsky, for example, describes Golyadkin by saying, "To live in the world would be quite unbearable for him; the black demon of his life, whom the hell of his insanity has transformed into a judge, is the pathological sensitivity and paranoia of his character."[2] Focusing on the "Mr. Hyde" who invades Golyadkin's "Dr. Jekyll," Belinsky defines Golyadkin's turmoil as the rise of a demonic judge who condemns from the start Golyadkin's every effort to find a place in the world. As the grim assessor becomes more and more powerful, he takes on a projected reality in the form of the double, who gradually eclipses every semblance of the "real" Golyadkin's personality. Finally, all that is left of Golyadkin is his psychosis.

More recently, Dyula Kirai has emphasized Golyadkin's social, psychological, and historical situation. In one article the Soviet critic states, "In *Dvoinik* Dostoevsky wanted to decipher a *social idea:* 'why people go out of their minds' ";[3] and in another piece we read,

> The theme of the novel *Dvoinik* turns out to be rooted precisely in a shifting social-psychological situation; the development of an *idée fixe* within that situation lies in the disclosure of the social-psychological causes of insanity for a person living under the condition of the 1840s.[4]

Steeped in the methods of Marxist criticism, Kirai begins and ends by viewing the novel as a mirror of a historical, social environment. Insisting that the work is commenting only on a person living in 1840s Russia, Kirai's approach bears no ramifications and harbors no threat for the modern critic. Here the interest is not so much in the living individual as in the social situation that supposedly shapes the individual; the accent is on the social phenomenon, not on the personal crisis.

Other modern critics have underscored the inner life of Golyadkin but without pursuing a connection between the life within and its relation to the other without. Natalie Reber, for instance, explains that the double comes to the surface as the result of "a dread nourished by the powers of guilt consciousness," which in turn leads to paranoia.[5] She is more concerned with Golyadkin's behavioral symptoms than with his discourse or response capability, and like Belinsky, she wrongly identifies the double as Golyadkin's judge (as for who his judges really are, that will be established in the discussion below). Finally, in a rather lame Freudian analysis of Golyadkin, Charles C. Hoffmaister claims that the double is not a persecutor of conscience but a success figure for the hero, whose "id freely expresses itself in impulsive, irrational behavior that precludes thought-directed action."[6] Unlike Lacan, Hoffmeister fails to go beyond the literalism of Freud's system; he ignores the fragmentation signified by the double as well as the concurrent breakdown in Golyadkin's response capability.

Because we are here dealing with a Lacanian analysis of language in regard to Golyadkin, such an analysis must be distinguished from a purely linguistic approach. In the most prominent example of a linguistic approach, V. V. Vinogradov, in his book on Russian naturalism, closely examines both the language of *Dvoinik* in general and Golyadkin's manner of speech in particular. He concludes that Golyadkin's discourse has a twofold purpose: "first, it provides a means of stating his intentions and sensations, and, secondly, it serves as the accompaniment peculiar to his actions." [7] Vinogradov, however, does not mention the structure of self or intersubjective relationships. The critic in this case has made the mistake of concentrating on Golyadkin without looking at the character's relation to the *other* and the way language characterizes that relation. The one thinker who addresses this matter is Mikhail Bakhtin; he has correctly understood that "Golyadkin's speech strives above all to simulate total independence from the word of the other." [8] Although Bakhtin does not develop this insight as much as he might, it will be helpful to refer to him in the ensuing analysis.

Lacan has said that "the Word imparts meaning to the function of the individual," [9] a remark that may guide our investigation of *Dvoinik,* for the loss of meaning and the onset of madness in Golyadkin's life are concurrent with his loss of the Word. To show that Golyadkin's madness is generated by a loss of the *parole,* I shall divide my remarks into three main sections: (1) the structure of the self; (2) the self and the other; and (3) judgment and the Word. These are the elements of Lacan's thinking that will take us the furthest in an analysis of Dostoevsky's *Dvoinik.*

The Structure of the Self

Lacan pictures the self as a dynamic of inter- and intrarelationships, as a structural *process,* which he represents in his simplified Schema L (see fig. 1, in chapter 3). It is easy to see how the Schema L may be used to describe Golyadkin. In

Dvoinik a person (S) occupies a dwelling in Saint Petersburg. He (a′) has a stake in establishing business and social relationships with certain people (a)—Andrey Filippovich and Anton Antonovich, for example. And there are those who serve as his judges (A), specifically Krest'yan Ivanovich and His Excellency. Bakhtin has, in fact, observed a similar structure of self in Golyadkin, claiming that his personality consists of three voices:

> His "I for myself" which is unable to do without the other and requires the other's recognition; his "I for the other" (his reflection in the other), that is, the voice which is Golyadkin's second substitute; and, finally, the voice of the Other who fails to acknowledge him and who at the same time has no real presence outside of him. [P. 372]

Applying the Schema L to Bakhtin's observations, we discover that Golyadkin's "I for myself" corresponds to Lacan's *moi* (a′), which seeks the recognition of the other through identification, through an effort to be like the other. His "I for the other" may be associated with Lacan's other (a), the alter ego or "second substitute" that commands the attention of the *moi*. And "the voice of the Other" closely parallels Lacan's Other (A), which signifies both the "significant Other" whom the individual appeals to and the internalization of this Other. Bakhtin and Lacan, then, have very similar notions of the self.

It must be noted, again, that the term "self" here denotes a process of inter- and intrarelation. "The 'who' of Dasein," to use Wilden's paraphrase of Heidegger, "is the shifter 'I,' which is a locus and not a person." [10] Moreover, says Heidegger, "Dasein approaches itself from that which concerns it," [11] so that whoever or whatever Golyadkin may be, he is structured by his relation to the other characters and by the way he perceives that relation. His longing for a place within the circle of the others is the longing of the self for itself. And the deeper the longing for acknowledgment, the greater the self's dependence on the other and the more severe the pending judgment. "The other is the indispensable mediator between me and myself," Sartre notes. "The very appearance of the other leads me to pronounce judgment on myself like an object, for it is as an object that I appear before the other." [12] Judgment, then, is an integral part of the process that constitutes the self.

The self as a process is a self as movement; insofar as Golyadkin is shaped by relation, he is shaped by action. To be sure, when he visits the doctor Krest'yan Ivanovich early in the novel, he stakes his claim to independence from others by explaining that even though he is "no master of eloquent speech," he compensates for it by being a man of action (p. 116). Thus, to use a phrase from Lacan's "Fonction," Golyadkin "makes an object of his action, but he does so in order to restore to it in due time its grounding function" (p. 285). Though he yearns for a relation, Golyadkin claims that he needs no support from others; instead, he cites his action as his support, so that his action becomes an object in itself. Yet in making this identification—that is, in making an object of his action—he is no longer engaged in action; he comes to a halt, and in doing so he loses the ability to speak. In his effort to justify himself, he is no master of speech, eloquent or otherwise, as is evidenced by his conversation with Krest'yan Ivanovich. Struggling to establish his selfhood, Golyadkin clings to the static groundwork of identity to avoid the ambiguity of process, in which he might create a self through the dialogical Word. Hence, in his effort to be himself he loses himself, since he is never able to engage in the action or to speak the Word that engenders the self. And so the seeds of madness are planted.

Michel Foucault has argued that "the function of the madman is to group all signs together in an endless proliferation of resemblance," [13] and resemblance begins with the mirror. Because he is more concerned with identity than with process, Golyadkin remains before the mirror, where he stands at the end of the novel's opening paragraph: "Although the sleepy, nearsighted, and rather bald figure reflected in the mirror was so insignificant by itself that at first glance it did not really command any special attention, its owner evidently remained quite satisfied with everything he saw in the mirror" (pp. 109–10). The reassuring satisfaction that the nearsighted Golyadkin derives from the "insignificant" reflection in the mirror reveals an element of the imaginary in his relation to the mirror. To the extent that the figure in the mirror is the only one whom he can trust, the mirror is a kind of lure sustained by the imaginary. Indeed, this is a characteristic of Lacan's *stade du miroir*. Wilden explains: "In studying what he called 'paranoiac knowledge,' Lacan formed the view that the paranoiac alienation of the ego through the *stade du miroir* was one of the preconditions of human knowledge. Thus the *moi* is essentially paranoid; it is 'impregnated with the Imaginary'" (p. 173). Golyadkin's self-satisfaction is not only self-delusion; it is self-division. The thing about himself that he finds so satisfying is not something within but an image in the glass, something unreal, void of substance. Already, in Golyadkin's attraction to the mirror, we discover the elements of "paranoiac alienation." Already we encounter the division of self marked by the double: here is the man and there the mirror image that displaces him. Cut in half, Golyadkin is a wounded man who leaves the mirror to visit the doctor Krest'yan Ivanovich; he hopes for a source of healing but fears he will find only a seat of judgment.

Thus from the very beginning one can see the "alienation of the ego" in Golyadkin's painful awareness of how he looks and of what is proper. He "assumes the appropriate countenance" (p. 114), for example, before entering the doctor's office, and he places an order in a restaurant purely for the sake of propriety (p. 123). He is preoccupied with showing that he is "like everyone else" (p. 135), and he dreads giving himself a bad name (p. 160): nothing must violate the imaginary form he longs to assume. And, of course, the harder he tries to be like others and to look proper, the more miserably he fails. Like the man in the Hasidic story who knew where his clothes were but could not find himself, Golyadkin has the look, the gesture, and the dress of the crowd, but he has no sense of himself as an individual. In short, he has no self.

Lacan offers an insight that applies very nicely at this juncture: "For in this labor by which the subject endeavors to reconstruct a construct *for another*, he discovers again the fundamental alienation which made him construct it *like another*, and which has always destined it to be stripped from him *by another*" (p. 249). The "construct" in this instance is the self Golyadkin longs to be, the one of whom it may be said, "He is his own man, like everyone else." But to be one's "own man" is not to be like everyone else, and this is an important aspect of Golyadkin's failure to be or to find himself. We see him torn between these poles when he declares that he wears no masks and plays no sycophantic games (p. 124), an assertion that is itself a mask. His assuming such a mask *for* another and *like* another is symptomatic of the psychosis brewing within him. Further, the facade may be stripped from him *by* another because the game he plays is a *language* game; the construct he sets up is a language construct, and this makes it a public matter. Because it is a public matter, it is alien to the Word, and this makes his language game self-alienating; instead of moving in the Word, he is stuck in the catchwords of *Das Man,* or "the They."

Here lies another touchstone in Lacan's "Fonction": "It is quite clear that the symptom is resolved entirely in an analysis of language, since it is itself structured like a language; for it is from language that the Word must be delivered" (p. 269). The difficulty for the self is to give voice to itself through the Word without losing itself to the objectifying constructs of language, without falling prey to the fixed formula that makes us like everyone else. If the self is a process, it is a process of speaking and responding; if the self is structured like language, it is structured according to its relation to the other. The idle talk and fixed phrases of the crowd are the opposite of the Word and preclude any response or relation to the other. For only the self who is at one with itself can be related to the other as an I related to a Thou; the self who is doubled or divided, fragmented by the discourse of the crowd, can generate no relation to the other.

The Self and the other

The relation between the self and the other lies in the relation between the language of the self and the language of *Das Man,*

or "the They." For *Das Man,* personal "reality" turns on identification within the coordinate system that comprises the
world; here the person sees as the other sees and speaks as the
other demands. In this way the language of *Das Man* provides
the individual with a *Man-selbst,* or a They-self, contoured to
fit into its proper slot in the crowd. The problem facing Golyadkin, then, is to accommodate himself to the categories of
the other without getting lost in those categories; that is, he
must speak the language of the other without slipping into a
mimicry of the other. He must talk without being lured into
idle talk; he must speak the language that relates him to the
other while retaining the Word, which is the language of the
self. And this is precisely what he cannot do. As soon as he
sets out to speak the language of truth and openness, the language of the self, he gets trapped in the script that *Das Man*
is forever following. And as the language of the self slips
away, madness sets in.

"In the case of the madman," Lacan writes, "the absence
of the Word manifests itself through the stereotypes of a discourse in which the subject, one might say, is spoken rather
than speaking" (p. 280). One way in which this occurs in *Dvoinik* is through Golyadkin's repeated use of popular phrases. He
often appends his remarks with the words "as they say" and
"as the saying goes" (for example, pp. 119, 120, 121, 125).
Indeed, Golyadkin is no master of eloquent speech and fre-
quently has trouble getting his words out at all, even to the
point of a virtual paralysis of the voice (for example, pp. 112,
124, 133–34). And, looking further, we never see Golyadkin
so irrevocably in the grips of the other as when he shrinks into
panicked flight upon encountering a colleague or a superior or,
at times, even his servant, Petrushka (pp. 112, 113, 124). A
slave to the language of the crowd, Golyadkin becomes a slave
to the other since freedom lies in the capacity to freely respond
with a word of one's own. Unable to respond to the other, he
is unable to win the recognition of the other and is left to com-
plete domination at the hands of the other.

If Golyadkin longs for a respectable position and a good
name, like everyone else, it is not exactly because he wants to

be like others or to fit into the crowd. Rather, as Lacan explains, the individual's desire "finds its meaning in the desire of the other, not so much because the other holds the key to the desired object, but because his primary object is to be recognized by the other" (p. 268). Prehaps the most revealing example of this is the fact that Golyadkin would sometimes dream of being in the company of distinguished and clever people, all of whom looked upon him with a favorable eye (p. 185). It is, however, just a dream; in reality Golyadkin's efforts to win the acclaim of others are at best fruitless, at worst destructive. And since he feels he is nothing without the recognition of the other, he ultimately reaches the point where he declares to himself, "There can be no doubt that I am ruined, that I have ceased to exist altogether" (p. 220).

In contrast to those critics who have wrongly identified the double as Golyadkin's judge, Bakhtin has accurately understood that "the basis of the plot lies in Golyadkin's attempt to find for himself a substitute for the other in the light of the utter lack of recognition of his self by others" (p. 368). This is where the double comes in; he is none other than the symbol or the personification of the conceptual other, what Foucault calls "the unthought" when he writes, "The unthought (whatever name we give it) is not lodged in man like a shrivelled-up nature or a stratified history; it is . . . the other that is not only a brother but a twin, born, not of man, nor in man, but beside him" (p. 326). The narrator of *Dvoinik,* in fact, refers to the double, in italics, as *drugoi,* or *the other* (p. 160). Golyadkin believes that the other, the double, is taking over his life, removing him from life, and this is just what it means to be both dominated and alienated by the other. Even in his dreams Golyadkin no sooner gains the recognition of the company surrounding him than the double appears and denounces him as the fraud he is (p. 186). From the moment he comes onto the scene, the double controls Golyadkin's every move to the point that Golyadkin cannot move at all. And because, as Lacan puts it, action "engenders the Word" (p. 271), the double's domination of Golyadkin's action amounts to a domination of the Word from Golyadkin's standpoint. It should also be noted that the discourse, or the *text,* that the double imposes on Golyadkin does not produce the imaginary relation—it controls it.

Thus we see that Golyadkin's lament that the double has imposed upon him the need to put everything into writing (pp. 175–76) is a lament over the loss of the Word. Writing, Derrida tells us, "menaces at once the breath, the spirit, and history as a revelation between self and spirit. It is their end, their finitude, their paralysis. Cutting short the breath, . . . it is the principle of death and difference." [14] Although Derrida intends this statement to be antilogocentric, we see that Golyadkin, frustrated by his failure to generate presence through the spoken Word, produces the written imprint that eclipses his voice. Unable to gain the spiritual presence embodied in the tone of the voice, he loses his voice to the atonal letter of the written word, the "letter written outside the man," as Saint Augustine calls it. [15] Just as when he stood before the mirror, Golyadkin now stands before the letter, gazing into the image that he continues to mistake for himself.

At this turn it should prove enlightening to consider the following observation concerning the *belle âme* from Wilden's essay on Lacan:

> The *belle âme* is a consciousness which judges others but which refuses action. In his vanity, the *belle âme* values his ineffective discourse above the facts of the world and expects it to be taken as the highest reality. . . . Thus the *belle âme* refuses the world and attains not being, but nonbeing, "an empty nothingness." . . . The *belle âme* fears the other because he wants so much to be the other, but being the other means losing himself. The whole paradox of identification is involved: seeking to be identical to the other, or seeking to possess the other's identity, is to lose one's own identity. [Pp. 289–90]

Golyadkin's longing both to be and not to be his double results in the loss of self because the all or nothing of identity or nonidentity precludes a relation to the other. Dominated, Golyadkin insists on dominating, and this produces a desire to be what he is not, a vain longing that adds to the fragmentation of self.

The self comes to itself by way of the other, and it creates a relation to the other by way of the Word. This is how we are to understand Lacan when he asserts:

> The form according to which language is expressed itself defines subjectivity. Language says, "You will go this way, and when you see that, you will turn there." To put it differently, language refers itself to the discourse of the other. It is enveloped as such in the highest function of the Word, insofar as the Word engages its author by investing the one to whom it is spoken with a new reality. [P. 298]

But Golyadkin seeks a new reality for himself without investing the other with a new reality; that is, he wants to be a greater human being without generating a relation with another human being. Like the *belle âme,* he is more concerned with identification than with relation, more interested in recognition than in response.

Golyadkin's one avenue to salvation lies in an appeal to an arbiter of truth, who occupies a third position between the other and himself, that is, between the double and himself. He must seek an audience, a *hearing,* in the presence of the Other, who, as Lacan explains, creates "the scene of the Word insofar as the scene of the Word is always in a third position between two subjects. This is simply to introduce the dimension of truth" (see Wilden, p. 269). Desperately hoping that his redeemer lives, Golyadkin seeks his redeemer in an attempt to regain his lost self, that is, in an effort to regain the Word. This brings us to our third item of concern.

Judgment and the Word

The doctor Krest'yan Ivanovich and the highest official Golyadkin works under, known as His Excellency, are the two main authorities of truth in the novel and as such represent the two figures of the Other. They are the two people from whom Golyadkin seeks a "diagnosis" or a response that will call him back to life. Let us consider, then, Golyadkin's relation to each of them.

It should first be noted that Golyadkin feels a need to communicate to Krest'yan Ivanovich something of the utmost importance, that he even thinks of the doctor as a kind of spiritual confessor (p. 113). The scene in the doctor's office, in fact, lays the groundwork for Golyadkin's loss of the Word and his degeneration into madness. It is here that Golyadkin's difficulty with words arises, along with his insistence that he is his own man. Yet apart from informing Golyadkin that he must change his life and his personality, the only significant reply Krest'yan Ivanovich gives Golyadkin is a series of long and "meaningful" intervals of silence (pp. 116–17). To be sure, Golyadkin continually meets with silence among his colleagues (p. 146) and even fears the silence of his servant (p. 144). So it is that in Golyadkin's attempt to speak, the first thing to make itself heard is the void, the trace of nothingness that outlines his tenuous presence.

In this regard Frederic Jameson has astutely called our attention to the fact that "the analyst's silence thus causes the structural dependency of the subject on the capital A of the Other's language to become visible as it never could in any concrete interpersonal situation." [16] Unable to speak the Word, Golyadkin is unable to elicit the Word from the doctor. Although he views the doctor as a confessor, he is entrenched in justification rather than confession. Instead of receiving a response that might absolve him, he meets with the silence that condemns him. For the silence of Krest'yan Ivanovich, again, points up the silent void, the absence of the Word, in Golyadkin himself.

Here the function of the Word in the psychoanalytic context begins to come into focus. Since "every Word calls for a reply," as Lacan says (p. 247), the Word makes a reply of the silence it encounters. The call of the Word and the silence of the void combine to establish the presence of the subject, a presence marked by what the subject is *not*. In his essay on Lacan, Wilden declares, "The subject *is* the binary opposition of presence and absence, and the discovery of One—the discovery of difference—is to be condemned to an eternal desire for the nonrelationship of zero, when identity is meaningless"

(p. 191). Unable to stand the weight of "being there" and the
opposition it entails, Golyadkin slowly becomes his own executioner, crying, "I am my own murderer!" (p. 180). For the
difference of presence and absence is just what Golyadkin cannot abide, and we see this in his desire to be his own man and
to control the other, by whom he is controlled; he believes that
if only he were in control, the difference that brings him into
a collision with nothingness would be eliminated. Impotent to
gain this upper hand, he proceeds to erect a monolith of narcissism. Hence the Word is reduced to an echo, and the self to
an image in the mirror.

Golyadkin's struggle to regain himself culminates in a frustrated return to the Other, which comes in the form of an attempt to regain a relationship with His Excellency. Aloof yet
dominating, His Excellency is the person whom Golyadkin
views as a father and to whom he makes his final appeal in the
name of the Father (p. 213). Though everyone else may fail to
acknowledge him, if Golyadkin can win the recognition of His
Excellency, then he can win redemption; then his existence
will be legitimate. He believes that an audience with His Excellency, the figure of the Law, will set everything straight and
restore him to his rightful self and to his proper place; the
confusion created by the double's takeover will be dispelled.
In this way he might win "the pardon of the Word," to borrow
Lacan's phrase (p. 281). Hence, in his would-be return to a
relation with the Word lie his longed-for redemption and salvation of self. And so he cries, "Your Excellency, I humbly
request your permission to speak" (p. 217).

But this attempt also meets with silence. Once again, because Golyadkin seeks redemption through justification, he
fails to respond and thus finds no response. In the final chapter
he is turned over to Krest'yan Ivanovich, who in the end is
much more than the Other as represented by the psychoanalyst; now he is the Other as god—or as devil. Now he is not
"the Krest'yan Ivanovich of before; this is another Krest'yan
Ivanovich! This is the terrible Krest'yan Ivanovich!" (p. 229).
It is significant that immediately before the doctor's arrival, a
silence falls over the gathering at the home of Berendeev, a

silence that Golyadkin takes to be an occasion for prayer (p. 227). For prayer is the most extreme form of the appeal of the Word to the Other; in prayer the intense absence created by silence makes most intense the precarious presence of the self. Thus Golyadkin comes before his last judgment only to be condemned by the doctor, whose last words are "severe and terrible, like a judge's sentence" (p. 229).

Conclusion

The foregoing analysis has shown that Golyadkin begins in a state of narcissism in which the Word is absent. Throughout the remainder of the novel he is engaged in a struggle to regain the Word and, with it, his self. As his efforts prove increasingly impotent, he sinks deeper and deeper into madness. Continually erecting walls around himself and attempting to cover all his bases, he entrenches himself more and more in a compromising position, and this is another indication of his removal from the Word. "To the extent that language becomes more functional," says Lacan, "it is rendered improper for the Word" (pp. 298–99). Golyadkin is ultimately lost in the functional in that he is irrevocably turned over to negotiation and justification. In short, he loves no one, and that is what his torment consists of. What is hell? It is the inability to love, says Zosima in *The Brothers Karamazov*.[17]

Still another indication that Golyadkin has lost the Word lies in his inability to make any response that he can call his own. Because, as we have seen, every Word calls for a reply, a relation to the Word is constituted by the ability to reply. And because Golyadkin can only parrot the discourse of the other, he cannot respond either to the other or to himself; such is the result of being locked into a struggle to win the recognition of the other. Thus captured by the other—the double—the imaginary eclipses the real, and Golyadkin is condemned by the Other.

What, then, has been gained by examining Dostoevsky's *Dvoinik* per Lacan's *parole?* First of all, Golyadkin cannot be dismissed as a Jekyll-and-Hyde whose schizoid personality is

aggravated by the appearance of the double. Secondly, his
madness cannot be unraveled by deciphering a "social idea,"
if that means reducing such insanity to a strictly social phenomenon. Further, Golyadkin's is not simply a case of chronic
angst, nor does he go mad over the appearance of the success
figure he could never become. What has been learned, with the
help of Lacan, is that this sort of investigation of the psyche
must at some point deal with the language of the psyche; *Dvoinik* reveals a connection between *speaking* oneself and *being*
oneself. That is to say, Lacan has enabled us to see the pri-
macy of language and the Word in the way in which we see
ourselves in relation to the world; we exist in a word-to-word
structure and not in a word-to-reality network. However accurate or well argued other studies of *Dvoinik* have been, they
have all failed to deal with this dimension of it. Thus Goethe's
reversal of Saint John—in the begining was the deed—is in
turn reversed: Lacan writes, "It was the *verbe* that was in the
beginning, and we live in its creation; but it is the action of
our spirit that continues this creation by forever renewing it"
(p. 271). Perhaps Buber says it best: "In the beginning was the
relation." [18]

I cannot conclude, however, without addressing the question of my personal relation to *Dvoinik* and its main character.
If I approach the novel as a critical curiosity or an an *object* of
analysis, then I have lost both the character and myself. It is
only by responding to the living voice of the novel that I can
generate a relation to it. Instead of isolating Golyadkin in
1840s Russia and maintaining the safety of objective distance,
I must find my way to Golyadkin by assessing myself in the
light of my assessment of him. Through the character, Dostoevsky summons me, and my relation to the character rests
on the response I offer. Having completed the analysis of
Dvoinik per Lacan's *parole,* I must shun the tempting illusion
that I have made a response and have established a relation.
To achieve a personal presence in relation to the novel, I must
address my life in the way I have addressed the life of Golyadkin; I must determine my existential stake in my critical activity. This means raising for myself the questions I have

raised for Golyadkin: What is the nature of my relation to the people around me? Is my discourse characterized by truthful and open response or by an effort to win recognition and domination? Am I preoccupied with looks, position, and self-justification, or is mine the language of response, embrace, and affirmation? And Dostoevsky himself reminds me that this last question is the one most needful. "You see," he writes, "I know that there is nothing higher than this thought of *embracing*." [19]

Religious Concepts of Language and Literature

IF PART ONE may be described as a general movement from religion toward literature, part two is largely a movement from literature toward religion. Again, however, it must be kept in mind that the linkage is circular; the dialogical Word, at work in both, makes literature religious and religion literary.

Chapter 5, "Mikhail Bakhtin and the Dialogical Dimensions of the Novel," examines in more detail the basis for dealing with the literary word in dialogical terms; it also clarifies why the dialogical Word may be regarded as the spiritual word. The point is that one need not go to a religious text such as Saint John's Gospel to unearth a religious concept of language. Literature itself entails such a concept, as indicated in Bakhtin's approach to the novel. Examining his approach, moreover, will shed more light, in retrospect, on Dostoevsky's novel *Dvoinik*. More than anywhere else, on Bakhtin's view the dialogical, and therefore the spiritual, dimensions of the novel unfold in the works of Dostoevsky.

Chapter 6 moves into a non-Christian area that nevertheless has some important Christian features. Like Christianity, Hasidism arose as a movement that de-emphasized the law and accented the presence of love in religious life. Both Martin Buber and Elie Wiesel, the two figures considered in chapter 6, pursue the relation between divine presence and the dialogical Word. But there is a significant difference: Wiesel takes up his pursuit of the dialogical Word through the dialogical medium of literature, while Buber, for the most part, operates within the more analytical tradition of philosophy. Buber's religious concept of language certainly has implications for a religious concept of literature, but Wiesel puts those implications into practice. In doing so, he brings to light the spiritual dimensions of the novel—and of life—evoked in Bakhtin's thinking.

Part two, then, is intended to add a dimension to, and thus fill out, an idea introduced in part one. I started with the ramifications for literary criticism of a religious concept of the Word; I now move to the ramifications for literary practice of a literary theory and a religious tradition.

CHAPTER FIVE

Mikhail Bakhtin and the Dialogical Dimensions of the Novel

IN HIS BOOK on Mikhail Bakhtin, Tzvetan Todorov describes the Russian thinker as "the twentieth century's greatest theoretician of literature."[1] Given its source, this recommendation alone is enough to consider what Bakhtin has to say and to ask of what value he might be to literary theory. His "ultimate value," as Wayne Booth expresses it, lies in his "full acknowledgement of and participation in a Great Dialogue."[2] Indeed, the concept of dialogue is central to Bakhtin's approach to literature in general and to the novel in particular. His own comment on the literary work best describes his own endeavor: "The work and the world represented in it enter the real world and enrich it, and the real world enters the work and its world as part of the process of its creation, as well as part of its subsequent life, in a continual renewing of the work through the creative perception of listeners and readers."[3] The dialogical dimensions of the novel draw readers into a dialogical interaction with the novel. At least one valuable aspect of Bakhtin's treatment of the novel is rooted in his bringing to light its dialogical dimensions through his own dialogical response, a response that has profound implications for how we view the novel.

This chapter shows how Bakhtin reveals that the novel is not simply a literary genre nor even an anti-genre, as Gary Morson has suggested,[4] but is more akin to a force, to use Donald Fanger's term.[5] The novel is a dynamic presence that characterizes the movement of response, the act of creation, and the search for truth. To be sure, Caryl Emerson has correctly observed that "Bakhtin's ultimate task" was "to make a unified truth compatible with multiple consciousnesses."[6] And in an unpublished paper titled "The Other Side of Bakhtin's Nineteenth Century: Reading Tolstoy in the Age of Dostoevsky," Emerson declares, "A unified truth made up of multiple consciousnesses is what Bakhtin meant by life." This is also how Bakhtin viewed the novel. Although Emerson, Fanger, Morson, Michael Holquist, and others have commented on Bakhtin's approach to the novel, none has brought out the connections linking responsive discourse, the creative act, and the expression of truth as dialogical dimensions of the novel and of life. In this chapter, then, I shall pursue these connections. Ultimately, my pursuit will lead to one more point revealed by Bakhtin but overlooked by his respondents: that the dialogical dimensions of the novel are the spiritual dimensions of the novel and of life itself.

Responsive Discourse

The novel does not consist of words and statements but rather is a combination of discourses and the responses to those discourses. For Bakhtin, moreover, word and discourse are of a piece; the Russian term *slovo,* in fact, embraces both of these notions.[7] But there is more to it than that. Emerson has claimed that Bakhtin "redefined the Word" by attempting "to infuse it with its original Greek sense of *logos* ('discourse')."[8] But this is not precisely the case. It is not the Greek sense of *logos* but the Johannine sense of *logos,* explained in chapter 2, that influenced Bakhtin's thinking on the Word, as a note from 1970–1971, contained in the collection of his works titled *Aesthetics of Verbal Art,* suggests: "Metalinguistics and the philosophy of the word. The ancient teaching of the *logos.* John."[9] As indicated in chapter 2, the Greek word *logos* may be translated as "reckoning," "explanation," "reason," "saying," "word," and so on; in more general terms, the Greek *logos* is at once thought and the expression of thought, simultaneously the idea and the manifestation of the idea. For Saint John, however, the *logos* is rendered as a living entity, as spirit, a *who* and not a *what;* for Saint John *logos* is life itself (1 John 1:1), and not one living thing has "its being but through him" (John 1:3).

Thus the Word, or discourse, in the novel is not to be distinguished from the life which it utters and which gives it utterance. And we recognize that life according to the world view that it articulates. For the Word, or discourse, as V. N. Voloshinov points out, embodies "*the ideological phenomenon par excellence.*"[10] Further, says Bakhtin in "Discourse in the Novel," a "particular language in a novel is always a particular way of viewing the world. . . . It is precisely as ideologemes that discourse becomes the object of representation in the novel" (see DI, p. 333). The *ideologeme* is the system of ideas that harbors a world view. The idea—that is, a manner of viewing, evaluating, and representing the world—is thus a primary ingredient of novelistic discourse.

To the extent that novelistic discourse includes an outlook *on* the world, it includes a consciousness *of* the world; and consciousness, in Heidegger's words, places us "before the world."[11] Consciousness situates the world "out there" and makes it a realm into which we venture and to which we respond. Yet the thing we respond to is not so much the world as a certain world view, and this response is what brings our own world view to life. "The idea begins to live," Bakhtin explains, "only when it enters into genuine dialogic relationships with other ideas. . . . The idea is a *live event,* played out at the point of dialogic meeting between two or more consciousnesses" (PDP, p. 88). Novelistic discourse rests on meeting or encounter, on coexistence and interaction; in the novel, being there entails being with. This is where Bakhtin's concept of the *chronotope* comes to bear; it is the critical juncture of space and time, the point where two consciousnesses encounter one another. Thus in "Forms of Time and the Chronotope in the Novel," he emphasizes the importance of the road, for example, as a chronotope in the novel (see DI, pp. 120, 248): the road, the path into the world, provides the place and the moment for the encounter between two beings, two ideas, two discourses.

The encounter between discourses is an encounter between word and alien word; this encounter gives life to discourse and to the Word. "The word," Bakhtin writes in "Discourse in the Novel," "is born in a dialogue as a living rejoinder within it; the word is shaped in dialogic interaction with an alien word" (DI, p. 279). The alien word is an alien ideology, a view and evaluation of the world that is not in keeping with one's own outlook. Wherever we encounter another consciousness, we encounter another word. Encounter in the novel—the contact between word and alien word—is a meeting of discourses from which each may emerge transformed by the other. This transformation characterizes "the activity of coming to know another's word," which, Bakhtin asserts in "Discourse in the Novel," is always included in the novel (DI, p. 353). If discourse in the novel is dialogical, then it is a discourse that includes the transformation of discourse, finding its life along the boundaries and at the thresholds of encounter.

Because encounter in the novel is encounter between discourses, Bakhtin points out in "From the Prehistory of Novelistic Discourse" that "language in the novel not only represents, but itself serves as the object of representation" (DI, p. 49). One cannot question a world view without questioning language. Further, language can become its own object of representation only when it includes a multiplicity of discourses, that is, only when it assumes the form of *polyglossia*, to use Bakhtin's term. As Todorov explains it, the novel "begins with a plurality of languages, discourses, and voices. The novel thus alters the consciousness of language and is self-reflective" (p. 104). Bakhtin's claim, however, is even stronger: "polyglossia and the *interanimation of languages* . . . made possible the genre of the novel" (DI, p. 50–51). Why? Because "only polyglossia fully frees consciousness from the tyranny of its own language and its own myth of language" (DI, p. 61). Polyglossia, or the multiplicity of languages, frees language—and with it, consciousness—by opening both to other languages and other consciousnesses. Polyglossia introduces to language a process of speaking and response and makes discourse responsive to the discourse of the other. In this interchange, discourse and idea come alive, and the language of the familiar and the language of the alien transform, and thus animate, one another.

Freeing consciousness from "the tyranny of its own language," polyglossia has a liberating impact on language, and a major indicator of that liberation is laughter. "Laughter," Bakhtin writes in a note from 1970–1971, "lifts the barriers and opens the way to freedom" (EST, p. 339). In the case of the novel, the barrier is that of official, authoritative language, the language of myth that characterized the epic. Along with polyglossia, therefore, Bakhtin cites laughter as the second of "two factors of decisive importance to the novel," arguing that laughter originally represents language through "the ridiculing of another's language and another's direct discourse" (DI, p. 50). Laughing at another's discourse—especially at authoritative discourse—is a means of deflating authority, of drawing near what had been distant, of unmasking what had been veiled and what had functioned as a veil. Hence laughter, and the "parodic-travesting forms" it assumed, "prepared the ground for the novel" by liberating the object of discourse from the net of authoritative language and destroying "the homogenizing power of myth over language." In this way, laughter "freed consciousness from the power of the direct word, destroyed the thick walls that had imprisoned consciousness within its own discourse" (DI, p. 60). In short, Bakhtin's "From the Prehistory of the Novel" demonstrates how laughter made language its own object of representation. Once the direct word—the word that endeavored to have the last word—had been robbed of its power, the dialogical word was free to pursue the creative act that gives birth to the novel.

The Creative Act

When the confines of a monological, formalized discourse are penetrated, consciousness is free to move beyond itself; it opens up to new discourse and thus to the creation of new

meaning. As Bakhtin points out in his notes from 1970–1971,
"Creation always goes with new meaning" (EST, p. 342), and
new meaning "exists only for other meaning" (EST, p. 350).
Creation requires encounter, the coupling or collision of one
discourse with another. Since other, or alien, meaning emerges
only through an encounter with alien discourse, the creation
of new meaning comes not only with the liberation born of
laughter but with the interaction born of polyglossia. The elements essential to the rise of the novel, then, are also essential
to the creative act, to the generation of meaning.

The creative act is a free act, and the freedom it enjoys is
the freedom to be other. In an early work titled "Author and
Hero in Aesthetic Activity," Bakhtin insists that the fundamental task facing the author is "to become *other* to himself,
to look upon himself through the eyes of another" (EST,
p. 16). And to look upon himself through the eyes of another
is to assume the discourse of another; here lies the transformation of the author as man into the author as creator. As
Emerson has noted in this regard, novels "grant freedom for
the *author* to develop, which is to say, freedom for the author
to play with his own image on the plane of his own work"
(Outer Word, p. 279). In "Forms of Time and the Chronotope
in the Novel" an extremely significant aspect of this movement
within the author is the development of the rogue, the clown,
and the fool—those who "are free to be 'other' in this world"
(DI, p. 159). Bakhtin argues that these three figures "influenced the positioning of the author himself within the novel
(and of his image, if he himself is somehow embedded in the
novel), as well as the author's point of view" (DI, p. 160). He
goes on to explain that "the novelist stands in need of some
essential, formal and generic mask that could serve to define
the position from which he views life, as well as the position
from which he makes that life public. And it is precisely here,
of course, that the masks of the clown and the fool (transformed in various ways) come to the aid of the novelist" (DI,
p. 161).

The rogue, the clown, and the fool thus play a major role
in the dialogical dimensions of the novel. They provide the

occasion for the encounter between word and alien word; they
set the scene for the free release of laughter. As the genre
which transforms discourse, the novel is the laughing genre,
which is to say that, in a sense, it is not a genre at all but a
movement, a force. This view of the novel is what lies behind
the importance that Bakhtin assigns to the Menippean satire in
the evolution of the novel. As he points out, "The 'inappropriate word'—inappropriate because of its cynical frankness,
or because it profanely unmasks a holy thing, or because it
crudely violates etiquette—is . . . very characteristic for the
menippea" (PDP, p. 118). The generation of truth or the creation of meaning is rooted in the inappropriate word. The inappropriate word is a form of the alien word, the word that
comes into collision with a standing discourse, an official *monologism,* that is, a "party line" or a ready-made truth. It sets
into motion the movement of dialogue that is essential to the
novel. As "the genre of 'ultimate questions'" (PDP, p. 115),
the Menippea combines laughter and polyglossia to enable the
author to put the needful question to himself and to his hero.
Questioning himself, he becomes other to himself.

   As the author becomes other to himself, he is able not only
to talk *about* the hero but to speak *with* the hero, so that he
can see and discover what the hero experiences. This process
is what constitutes the aesthetic event as an encounter between
discourses, between consciousnesses, where "the consciousness of the author," we read in "Author and Hero," "stands in
a relation to the consciousness of the hero—not from the
standpoint of his thematic composition or thematically objective significance but from the standpoint of his living subjective unity" (EST, pp. 79–80). And the hero's living subjective
unity lies in a discourse he can call his own, free from the
discourse and ideology of the author. Again, it is discourse in
dialogue with discourse that forms the root and branch of the
author's relation to the hero. The result of this dialogue is character, where "by *character* we mean that form of interrelation
between hero and author which carries out the task of creating
a whole hero as a defined personality" (EST, p. 151). Thus
when novelistic discourse is viewed in dialogical terms, the

notion of character takes on a dynamic quality: the character is an *event,* and not a static entity whom we can file into a predetermined category.

The dynamic view of character is of particular importance in Bakhtin's treatment of Dostoevsky. In *Problems of Dostoevsky's Poetics,* he writes that, with respect to character, self-consciousness "presupposes a radically new *authorial position* with regard to the represented person. . . . At issue here is precisely the discovery of a *new integral view on the person*—the discovery of . . . 'the man in man' (Dostoevsky)—possible only by approaching the person from a correspondingly new and *integral* authorial position" (pp. 57–58). The essential element in the integral authorial position, as well as in the integral view of the person, is consciousness of self, or the self's relation to itself; indeed, the self is precisely its relation to itself. Consciousness of self is achieved in the movement toward the discourse of the other, whereby I become other to myself; here I behold myself through the eyes of another and lend an ear to my own discourse through the resonance of the other's discourse.[12] Yet as soon as this occurs, the image of myself as other, as Bakhtin puts it in "Author and Hero," "immediately becomes a feature of the inwardness (experienced) of my life" (EST, p. 77). This is how the author approaches the "man in man" within himself and within the hero, thus bringing an integral view to both; each enters the novel in a responsive, dialogical manner.

Whether author or hero, the integral man is the opposite of the hollow man. It must be emphasized, however, that, since what is outwardly perceived is immediately internalized, the integral view is not something completed but is rather something steeped in "*that internally unfinalizable something in man*" (PDP, p. 58). The dialogical movement—the leap outward and back inward—is unending. Another way of expressing this point is to say, with Lacan, that "every Word calls for a reply."[13] Filling out this thought, in Bakhtin's "The Problem of Verbal Genres" we read, "Every understanding of living speech, of living expression, bears an actively responsive character" (EST, p. 247). Along with its antecedent, every word has its uttered or unuttered response, so that *"nothing conclusive has yet taken place in the world, the ultimate word of the world and about the world has not yet been spoken"* (PDP, p. 166). If we connect this idea with the following statement, perhaps we can see the link between self-consciousness and open-endedness as dialogical dimensions of the novel: "Self-consciousness, as the *artistic dominant* governing the construction of character, cannot lie alongside other features of his image; it absorbs these other features into itself as its own material and deprives them of any power to define and finalize the hero" (PDP, p. 50). It is not only what we find in the novel that makes it open-ended but what goes into its creation; the author's consciousness of himself is mediated by his relation to the hero and is essential to the creation of the hero. Consciousness of self, then, is not a trait—it is an activity, a process of listening and response. If traits serve to define and to confine, self-consciousness serves to liberate, to release into the open.

The terms self-consciousness and open-endedness parallel the terms laughter and polyglossia. The ability to laugh at oneself accompanies an awareness of oneself; polyglossia generates an open-ended proliferation of discourse; and the proliferation of discourse turns back to enhance self-consciousness. It should also be pointed out that in the concepts of self-consciousness and open-endedness we have the fundamental aspects of the polyphonic novel, which, in Bakhtin's words, *"is dialogic through and through"* (PDP, p. 40). But polyphony is not a characteristic of Dostoevsky's novels alone, as one might gather from a reading of Bakhtin's book on Dostoevsky. Polyphony is a feature of the evolving novel itself, as Bakhtin himself indicates in "The Problem of Text in Linguistics, Philology, and Other Humanistic Sciences": "since Dostoevsky, polyphony has firmly established itself throughout world literature" (EST, p. 291). The important point here is not that polyphony distinguishes Dostoevsky's novels but that it has come to distinguish the novel in all its dialogical dimensions. Simply identifying polyphony as a system of languages, however, is not enough. The next step is to determine exactly what this dialogical dimension of the novel means to language and the Word, what it means to truth and presence.

Dialogical Truth and Dialogical Presence

It will be recalled from the discussion of Lacan in chapter 3 that in his commentary in Lacan's *The Language of the Self,* Anthony Wilden cites a statement by Lacan suggesting that his concept of *Otherness* may be rendered by the term *Thirdness.* "The Other with a big 'O,'" said Lacan, "is the scene of the Word insofar as the scene of the Word is always in third position between two subjects. This is only in order to introduce the dimension of Truth" (p. 269). This remark from Lacan may help one understand Bakhtin's notion of the "third position" and how that notion is related to the open-endedness of dialogical discourse and dialogical truth. His concept of the "loophole left open" is a good place to start. Consider, for example, the following passage: "This potential other meaning, that is, the loophole left open, accompanies the word like a shadow. Judged by its meaning alone, the word with a loophole should be an ultimate word and does present itself as such, but in fact it is only the penultimate word and places after itself only a conditional, not a final, period" (PDP, p. 233). The potential other meaning points up an implicit third position, distinct from the positions of speaker and listener or author or reader. A word cannot be assessed on the basis of its dictionary meaning but only within the realm of discourse that surrounds any given intersubjective exchange and which leaves the possibility of new meaning open-ended.

This third position, moreover, leaves open the prospect of an unrealized, unfinalized truth, in contrast to the ready-made truths and fixed formulas of monologism. Here we would do well to recall what Bakhtin says about truth and the novel's dialogical concern with truth:

> At the basis of the genre [of the novel] lies the Socratic notion of the dialogic nature of truth, and the dialogic nature of human thinking about truth. The dialogic means of seeking truth is coun-

terposed to *official* monologism, which pretends to *possess a ready-made truth*. . . . Truth is not born nor is it to be found inside the head of an individual person, it is born *between people* collectively searching for truth, in the process of their dialogic interaction. [PDP, p. 110]

Truth is a distinguishing dialogical dimension of the novel, and it lies more in process than in outcome, more in seeking than in finding. That which is finalized in the author or in the reader is never the truth; rather, the truth forever abides in an open-ended, unfinalized third position outside of speaker and listener.

Bakhtin's "The Problem of Text in Linguistics, Philology, and Other Humanistic Sciences" contains passages that may shed some light on this matter. Let us first examine the following: "Every dialogue proceeds as though against the background of a third who is invisibly present, standing above all the participants in the dialogue. . . . The third referred to here has nothing to do with mysticism or metaphysics . . . it is a constitutive feature of the whole expression" (EST, p. 306). The *third* represents the horizon of possibility of the multiplicity of responses that might be offered in the dialogue; as possibility—or the One for whom all things are possible—the *Third* sustains the movement of the dialogue. Truth is always open to discussion, is always open-ended; there can be no final, definitive response to a novel. What is more, each response offered in a dialogue expands the horizon of the Third, so that the dialogue bears a proliferation of possibility. The response offered by one interlocutor transforms the discourse of the other, and the Third position shifts.

Thus the Word, says Bakhtin in "The Problem of Text," is "transindividual":

> The Word (any sign in general) is transindividual. Everything said or expressed lies outside the 'soul' of the speaker and does not belong to him. . . . The author (speaker) has his inalienable rights to the Word, but his rights are also the listener's rights; his rights are the rights of those whose voices resound in the Word offered by the author. . . . The Word is a drama in which three characters participate (not a duet but a trio). [EST, pp. 300–301]

The author in question is not Adam, not the first to breach the silence of the universe. His every utterance, his every scrawl, is replete with a host of words within the Word. Likewise, the listener, whose hearing is tinted with the discourse that shapes his world view, must sift through not only the author's word but those voices that echo in the author's word as well as in his own ideology. This sifting and analyzing points up the reader's active role.

At least one question suggests itself in the light of Bakhtin's comments on the third position: Who is speaking? To be sure, Holquist has deemed this "the obsessive question at the heart of Bakhtin's thought" (p. 307). Foucault tells us that Mallarmé responded to the question of who is speaking by answering, "The being of the word itself." [14] To this we might add Heidegger's remark that "language speaks. Man speaks to the extent that he responds to language." [15] Citing these statements might make more clear some of the implications of Bakhtin's insights. We discover, first of all, that if *Ulysses,* for example, was written by James Joyce, the breath that gave it life came from an atmosphere of language consisting of a multitude of discourses. The notion that it is language or the Word that speaks in the novel also underscores an important Bakhtinian distinction, namely the difference between the author as man and the author as creator. The authorial voice heard in the novel is not simply that of the man but that of the man drawing on the language of creation, the language of collision between word and alien word; the one who speaks may be he who responds to language but language itself also speaks. When language becomes its own object of representation—as it does in the novel—language speaks, reveals itself. Viewed dialogically, the language of a novel resides neither in the novelist nor in the reader but in a system of discourses above the two. And since the novel's language system is open-ended, its word is never the last word nor its meaning the ultimate meaning. "A word uttered," Bakhtin declares in "Author and Hero," "is the dead flesh of meaning" (EST, p. 117). Meaning slips through the holes in the net of language, and the spirit is drained off in the utterance; the spirit is always somewhere else, in third position. Like living truth, meaning is alive only when it is still outstanding, only when it is yet to be.

Only when it is yet to be . . . at this point one should recall Bakhtin's observations on the relation between meaning and time. In "Author and Hero," for example, we read, "All temporality, all duration, confronts meaning as *yet-to-be-fulfilled,* as something incomplete, as *not-all-over-yet"* (EST, p. 107). Meaning is future oriented. To borrow an image from Nikolai Gogol, it dwells in the realm where the troika has yet to arrive. It lies just beyond the threshold, on the other side of the next tick of the clock. Regarding the novel, this suggests that, given its dialogical dimensions, it is forever incomplete as a form. The same implication applies to author and reader, indeed, to anyone who says, "I." Listen to Bakhtin: "The definition given to me lies not in the categories of temporal being but in the categories of the *not-yet-existing,* in the categories of purpose and meaning, in the meaningful future, which is at odds with anything I have at hand in the past or present. To be myself for myself means yet becoming myself" (EST, p. 109). Everywhere Bakhtin employs the first-person pronoun in this citation from "Author and Hero," he could well have used the term *novel.* Because of its dialogical dimensions, the novel exists in the categories of the not-yet-existing; for the novel, being means being in the process of becoming.

The novel brings to literature "a certain semantic openendedness," as Bakhtin expresses it in "Epic and Novel," "a living contact with unfinalized, still evolving contemporary reality (the openended present)" (DI, p. 7). The open-ended present is dialogical presence, presence in motion, moving ahead, as the phrase "still evolving" suggests; that phrase orients the novel—just as it orients meaning—toward the future. Hence the novel, viewed in its dialogical dimensions, is not the *vessel* of meaning but the *carrier* of meaning, and its orientation toward the future is precisely what establishes its contact with the ever-shifting present. The word *living* is also important to an understanding of the novel's contact with the present. Because its bond with the present is a living bond, the novel is a living, polyphonic voice, an "I" consisting of a legion of "I's." The address to the reader, the authorial word that speaks, the ideologies that frame the context, the discourses that precede the work—all of these go into the novel's voice and fill out its dialogical dimensions; all of these instill the novel with a dialogical presence that is forever fulfilled yet never finished.

As for the novel's contact with the past—its memory, so to speak—here too we find open-ended orientation, which is quite distinct from the epic's relation to an ancient or absolute past. Once again, Lacan may help, for what he says of the "I" in the following statement may also be said of the novel: "What is realized in my history is not the past definite of what I was . . . but the future anterior of what I shall have been for what I am in the process of becoming" (p. 63). There is a similar remark, though more cryptic, in Bakhtin's "Author and Hero": "For the 'I,' memory is memory of the future" (EST, p. 110). Again, the first-person pronoun here may also be applied to the novel as a living voice. The past discourses out of which the novel is born shape the form it will have assumed in the future. This is not to imply anything like a predetermined direction or a cause-and-effect plotting of where the novel is headed; any single direction that its evolution may follow derives from an open horizon of possibility that is contoured by the past and oriented toward the future. The mindfulness of the past discourses is a mindfulness of the future, of what the novel is coming to be. And this mindfulness is what brings the novel into contact with the present, what characterizes its dialogical presence. For the novel's presence, like the presence of any living voice, is dialogical and thus rests on the word still unspoken, on the discourse yet to be.

Conclusion: The Spiritual Dimensions of the Novel

According to Bakhtin's thinking on the dialogical dimensions of the novel, the novel is a polyphonic voice that responds to a world of voices, and not a mirror that reflects a standing reality. It is created through a process whereby an "I" becomes "other," through the collision and encounter between word and word. Open-ended and ever-changing, the novel lives in the tension of speaking and response, present in the polarity and not at the poles, continually renewed by the dialogical search for an unfinalizable truth.

Couched in Bakhtin's views on the dialogical dimensions of the novel—particularly in his thinking on the "third position," dialogical truth, and dialogical presence—is a sense of the spiritual dimensions of the novel; indeed, the novel's dialogical dimensions are precisely its spiritual dimensions.[16] Any word about Bakhtin's thinking on the novel, therefore, would remain incomplete without a word about the religious nature of his thought. More than anywhere else, this religious element and its dialogical aspects are revealed in the selections found in *Aesthetics of Verbal Art*, especially in the early essay "Author and Hero." There he asserts, for example, that "*to cease becoming . . . means spiritual death*" (p. 109). And: "The soul is the gift of my spirit to the *other*" (p. 116), where such giving characterizes the process of becoming; if there is no giving, there is no becoming. Spiritual life is rooted in the offering of the soul to the other, and the substance of that offering is the Word. In Bakhtin's thinking, there is an affinity between Word and spirit; as long as I continue to offer my word in dialogical response, I continue to live spiritually, for this is the offering that constitutes my becoming. Bakhtin might, in fact, go so far as to say, with Buber, that "spirit in its human manifestation is man's response to his You. . . . It is not like the blood that circulates in you but like the air in which you breathe. Man lives in the spirit when he is able to respond to his You."[17] The novel is just such a response, and our relation to the novel is grounded in such a response. The greater the response, the greater the gift offered and received; the greater the response capability, the greater the ability to become.

As the gift of the spirit to the other, the soul, conceived in Bakhtinian terms, has implications for the relation between author and hero. If the author's task in creating the hero is to become other to himself, he must experience the internal life of the hero as soul; to bring his hero to life, he must offer the innermost part of his own life to the hero. But as soon as the hero comes alive, he, like a living individual, enters into the process of relating himself to himself; he becomes unfinalized, turned over to the categories of the not-yet-existing. At that point, says Bakhtin, "the life of the hero begins to struggle to break through form and rhythm. . . . An artistically convincing completion becomes impossible; the soul of the hero shifts from the category of *other* to the category of *I*—it disseminates and loses itself in spirit" (EST, p. 116). When this occurs, we are able to receive the gift of the hero's word, and we receive his word by responding to it, by offering our own word.

As it goes with the hero, so it goes with the novel as an incomplete, ever-evolving presence, a presence or force characterized by its dialogical dimensions. It is said that each novel has a soul of its own, but as soon as its voice flows into the sea of voices, its word disseminates into spirit. It is from the depths of spirit and Word that the art summons us to respond and thus engage in the dialogue that instills us with spiritual life and sustains the process of becoming. This dialogical endeavor, this struggle to respond, is what distinguishes Bakhtin's life and his offering to life. We began with Wayne Booth's acknowledgement of Bakhtin's participation in a "Great Dialogue"; perhaps we would do well to end with a thought that marks the beginning of Bakhtin's participation in the Great Dialogue and underscores what lies behind that participation; it is from his first published work, "Art and Responsibility": "I must respond with my life for what I have experienced and understood in art. . . . Art and life are not one and the same, but they must become one in me, in the wholeness of my responsibility" (EST, pp. 5–6). The work of art opens up life's dialogical dimensions, and we are instilled with life to the extent that we move within those dimensions. Bakhtin thus brings ethical and religious implications to aesthetics. If Kierkegaard divided these three aspects into stages along life's way, Bakhtin transformed them into dialogical dimensions of life itself.

CHAPTER SIX

The Apotheosis of Presence:
Buber, Wiesel, and Hasidism

IN CHAPTER 5 I examined the dialogical dimensions of the
novel as the spiritual dimensions of the novel. It was shown
how a religious philosophy of language and the Word may lend
itself to an expression of a religious theory of literature. In this
chapter I shall examine a religious philosopher and a literary
figure in the light of another religious tradition. As with Bakhtin, the accent here is on relation between Word and presence,
between tale and reality. Let us consider, then, this ontological
interplay between religious philosophy and religious literature
and see what light it may shed on a religious concept of language and literature.

The eighteenth century was just blinking its eyes at the dawn
of the Enlightenment when an orphan named Israel ben Eliezer
(1700–1760) became an assistant to a teacher of young children in the East European province of Podolia. It is said that
one day, instead of conducting them to school in the usual,
dutiful manner, he led the little ones to their studies in a procession of song.[1] Thus the ignition of the flame of joy and
fervor known as Hasidism, a movement that endeavored to
overcome despair with dance and sorrow with song.

Israel ben Eliezer, or the Baal Shem Tov ("Master of the
Good Name"), turned Judaism from a cry of "How long, oh
Lord?" to an affirmation of the moment, bridging the gulf be-
tween heaven and earth. "If I love God," he once asked,

93

"what need have I of a world to come?"[2] The Hasidic focus
on presence, on the presence of God in man's love for God,
has left its indelible mark on two of the twentieth century's
most profound thinkers: Martin Buber and Elie Wiesel. Buber
has described Hasidism as a form of mysticism that hallows
time and sanctifies the moment.[3] He tells us, for example, that
when a Hasidic student was asked what his departed teacher's
greatest concern had been, the young man replied, "Whatever
he was engaged in at the moment" (*Botschaft,* p. 778). Similarly, Wiesel has asserted, "Such is the nature of Hasidism:
the accent is on presence."[4] And in *Somewhere a Master* we
read, "God is in His creation—God is present, God is presence. It is up to man to be present, too—present to God, to
himself, and to his fellow man."[5] Both Buber and Wiesel,
then, are mindful of the Shekhina, of God's Presence and In-
dwelling, in this moment, in this person, in this event.

Despite this important similarity, however, there are significant differences between these two thinkers and their relations
to Hasidism. Buber, it will be noted, is generally known for
his philosophy, whereas Wiesel is generally known for his
literature. Buber systematically outlines what he regards as
the four essential elements of Hasidism: *hitlahavut* (ecstasy),
avoda (service), *kavanna* (intention), and *shiflut* (humility).
Wiesel, on the other hand, turns his attention to the soul on
fire and to the Hasidic struggle with despair. Buber compiled
the tales and legends of the Hasidim and incorporated their
teachings into works such as *Ich und Du* (I and Thou) and
Zwiesprache (Dialogue); Wiesel has woven the Hasidic legends into his own tales. Nearly all of Buber's Hasidic works
date from before the Holocaust; all of Wiesel's writings have
been generated out of the Holocaust. While Buber turned to
Hasidism by turning away from mysticism and its isolation,
Wiesel returned to Hasidism, the religion of his childhood, but
with a difference—his return was an effort to resurrect some
embrace of life from the ashes of death.

The end of Buber's mysticism came with a now famous in-
cident. A young man, a student, came to him for help. Uncon-
cerned with the affairs of this world, Buber did not offer the

help sought. Not long afterward the student committed suicide. The young man's death summoned Buber to life and to Hasidism. A terrible tale indeed, but how much more so is Wiesel's story of the experiences in the camps, related in *Night?* Shall we say, then, that Buber encountered Nothingness, while Wiesel collided with it? That for Buber the apotheosis of presence means recognizing God *in* the moment, while for Wiesel it means resurrecting God *to* the moment? There does seem to be more of the mountain of fire and the leap into the abyss about Wiesel's relation to Hasidism; like the Great Maggid of Mezeritch (d. 1772), he seeks his passion among the ashes (see *Souls,* p. 71). But let us not be too quick to weigh the calm of the philosopher against the cry of the artist. For concern with Hasidism and its legends lends a literary element to Buber's philosophy, just as it imparts a philosophical dimension to Wiesel's literature. Both are men of letters—no, both are men of the Word: like an I answering a Thou, each responds as he is beckoned, from the depths of passion, the depths of deep calling to deep.

Here lies the key to the revelation of God out of the moment at hand, the key to the apotheosis of presence: it is a transformation effected by the power of the Word, by the relation of I and Thou, and by the movement of passion. Let us, then, consider how these dimensions of the apotheosis of presence find their Hasidic expression in the philosophy and literature of Buber and Wiesel.

The Power of the Word

In *Mein Weg zum Chassidismus* (*My Path to Hasidism*), Buber tells us, "For Hasidic teaching, the entire world is but a word from the mouth of God." [6] The world comes into being and is sustained by the fiat: let there be. . . . This is the Word uttered in the beginning, and presence means that now is the beginning. On the Hasidic view, everything begins; nothing ends. The Word sets into motion the movement of the beginning, the movement over the face of the deep; it harbors not only the

mystery of creation but the void from which creation arises.
Buber describes what this is like:

> The Word is an abyss through which the speaker strides. "Words
> should be spoken in such a way that heaven might open up in
> them. And not as if you take the Word into your mouth, but as if
> you were entering into the Word." He who is acquainted with the
> hidden song that transports the inner into the outer, who is famil-
> iar with the holy round that fuses the lone, delicate Word to the
> song of the distances—he is filled with the power of God, "and it
> is as if he created heaven and earth and the entire world anew." [7]

And in *The Gates of the Forest,* Wiesel declares, "In taking a
single word by assault it is possible to discover the secret of
creation, the center where all threads come together." [8] To enter the Word is to enter creation through creation. As we create
through the Word, we are created by the Word; as we summon,
we are summoned.

The power of the Word thus lies in the power to beckon. It
rises from the deep to summon from the depths; it calls us
forth, into presence, into being. In short, the power of the
Word is the power of God. "Man is involved with the Creator," writes Abraham Heschel, "by his very being; for in being
he obeys the command, 'Let there be!' Just to be is holy." [9]
The ability to hear the Word's call to being, moreoever, is
rooted in the ability to respond; says Buber, "He who no
longer responds to the Word no longer hears the Word." [10] Nor
do we have to wait around for the summons to come; this attitude of waiting only points up our deafness, for the summons
is here, in the situation at hand. And the call that rises up from
the moment—a call that comes from us and from beyond
us—is what constitutes any situation as a *living* situation. "It
demands nothing of what has been," Buber explains. "It demands presence, responsibility; it demands you." [11] In *Vom
Leben der Chassidim (On the Life of the Hasidim)* he asserts
that "from all the things of the earth" the eye of God "catches
the glance of the one who seeks" (p. 25); it may be added that
the voice of God reaches the ear of the one who listens and,

with Buber, that "every being is the fruit through which He offers Himself to the longing soul" (p. 25).

Quoting a Hasidic master on the same subject, Wiesel writes: "The road to God goes through man. The sleeping child, the mother caressing him, the old man listening to the rustling of the leaves; God is close to each of them, in each of them God is present" (*Souls,* p. 208). God is present in the child, in the mother, in the old man, because the Word beckons us through each of them. Any relationship a person has with God rests on his or her relationship with the people; the Word of God, his summons, is the Word that calls through the mouths of babes and men and women. As we respond to them, we respond to God, and whatever presence we may have is attained by becoming one with the Word we pronounce. "A good speaker," said the Maggid of Mezeritch, "must become one, not with his audience, but with his words; the moment he hears himself speak, he must conclude" (*Souls,* p. 71). For as we hear ourselves speak, we step outside ourselves and thus lose our presence; we are no longer here but there, lost in the calculations and convolutions of the words we utter. Such preoccupation with how we sound or look marks the beginning of the first brick in the wall that cuts us off from ourselves, and from others, and therefore from God.

Presence is the opposite of this fragmentation; presence is made of that which is hale, hallowed, and whole. This is what it means to assert that God is one: there is but one presence. "For all things above and below," Buber teaches, "are a *single* unity. 'I am the prayer,' speaks the Shekhina. A zaddik said, 'Men believe they pray before God, but this is not so, for the prayer itself is divinity' " (*Leben,* p. 29). Prayer is divinity, because prayer is presence, the place where the Word finds its full presence. No prayer can be uttered half heartedly, half-sincerely, half-passionately; and all prayer is more in the nature of quest than in the nature of request. More than anywhere else, in prayer we are one with the Word, for the prayer is at once a response to the Word and a vessel of the Word. And as we become one with the prayer, the prayer becomes one with

God. "I no longer ask You to resolve my questions," Wiesel cries, "only to receive them and make them part of You." [12]

Becoming one with the Word we speak, we become the language of God; indeed, Wiesel hails the word of Menahem Mendl of Vitebsk (d. 1788), "Man is the language of God," as the most beautiful phrase the rebbe ever pronounced (*Souls*, p. 86). This statement is an affirmation of the Word that draws man and God together to form a single, living presence. That Buber makes no mention of this remark in his *Erzählungen der Chassidim* (*Tales of the Hasidim*) is significant to the differences between him and Wiesel, between the philosopher and the novelist. Man is the language of God only when present within a living situation, and as a storyteller, Wiesel struggles to breathe life into a given situation. Here the artist neither describes nor analyzes nor imitates—he creates through the power of the Word; his purpose is not to explain but to engage, to bring his witness before the countenance, to make present. Thus we pray with Michael at the wall, we stand with Gregor at the gates of the forest, and we go with Paltiel on his quest for the Messiah. This is where one hears the intonations and the nuances of the language of God, something not always heard in the analysis and explanation that characterize Buber's approach to Hasidism.

Consider, for example, Buber's treatment of Rebbe Nahman of Bratzlav (d. 1810) with respect to the Word. Pursuing his philosophical interest in the relation between I and Thou, Buber focuses on Nahman's similar concern with the Word and emphasizes the latter's remark that "he who receives the Word of his neighbor also receives his own soul and is therein awakened." [13] Buber goes on to explain that the decisive thing for Nahman is the Word's effect "not on the speaker but on the listener" (p. 903). Again, the only Word we have from God is the Word spoken now, by the person here before me, for that person is the language of God. To be sure, the power of the Word to awaken its auditor must be noted in this regard, but it should also be pointed out that Buber's concern with Nahman lies in what the rebbe can add to a philosophical understanding of the I-Thou relation. His interest is in Nahman the thinker, not in Nahman the storyteller, as he is known to the Hasidim.

Wiesel, on the other hand, is a teller of tales, and this is reflected in his approach to Nahman:

> "It is written," Rebbe Nahman says, "that the Just Men obey the word of God. This should be read differently: Just Men make the word of God." A literal translation, which on the Master's lips means: Just Men compose the language with which God creates His universe. Prophets transmit the word of God, Just Men conceived it. Often in the form of tales.
>
> Every word is a tale, they said in Bratzlav. Example: Torah. Or Talmud. Or Zohar. The tale of the Law is as important as the Law. And it is more profound than its commentaries. [*Souls,* p. 187]

Where Buber offers a commentary, Wiesel offers a tale. Wiesel's accent on the power of the Word within the context of the tale becomes clearer still when he relates a Hasidic legend both in *Souls on Fire* (pp. 167–68) and in the Preface to *The Gates of the Forest*. It seems that when the Baal Shem saw misfortune threatening the Jews, he would go to a certain place in the forest, where he built a fire, said a prayer, and the miracle needed was accomplished. Later, when the Maggid of Mezeritch was faced with the same task, he would go to the same place in the forest and cry, "Master of the Universe! I do not know how to light the fire, but I know the prayer." Again the miracle was accomplished. Still later, on similar occasions, Moshe Leib of Sassov (d. 1807) would go into the forest and say, "I do not know how to build the fire, nor do I know the prayer; but I know the place." And that was enough to bring about the miracle. Finally, it fell to Israel of Rizhin (d. 1850) to achieve a miracle. Sitting at home, his head in his hands, he spoke to God: "I cannot light the fire; I do not know the prayer; I have even lost the place in the forest. All I can do is tell the tale." And this was sufficient.

In *Le mendiant de Jérusalem* (*A Beggar in Jerusalem*), David proclaims, "In the beginning was the Word; and the Word is the story of man; and man is the story of God." [14] The

language of God is the language of the tale, and if the Word
makes man the language of God, it makes God the tale of man.
God created man, say the Hasidim, because he loves stories;
the Word that was in the beginning is literary in essence. It is
the presence of God and man in the Word, moreover, that
makes the Word the vessel of presence, and where there is
presence, there is apotheosis. For presence is constituted by
the Word's conjunction of the human and the divine as I and
Thou, and the tale is where this conjunction occurs.

The Relation of I and Thou

The notion that God abides in this event, in this object, in *this
human being* is fundamental to Hasidism. Says Buber: "Man
cannot draw near to the divine by reaching beyond the human
. . . but only by becoming human; to become human is what
he, this individual man, has been created for. This strikes me
as the eternal core of Hasidic life and Hasidic teaching." [15]
Further, the path to God does not lead through the mass of
people but through this single human being now before me.
How to love God? Love the person before you. How to love
this person? Love God. The two acts of loving are inseparable.
There is but a single love, a single event, a single presence.
And if it should be said that another is not always before us, I
shall answer that only the I is subject to absence—the Thou is
always there. If we find ourselves alone, it is because we have
failed to hear, not because another has failed to call.

It is evident that Buber's most famous work, *Ich und Du,* is
not simply the product of philosophical rumination; it bears
the mark of Hasidism as well. Recall, for example, the following insight from the piece: "We cannot find God by remaining
in the world; we cannot find God by departing from the world.
Whoever goes forth to his Thou with the whole of his being
. . . will find the One who cannot be sought." [16] What cannot
be found at either pole rises up in the polarity. Who is the One
who cannot be sought? Presence, which is always a *who* and
never a *what*, for presence dwells only in the polarity, in the
relation of I and Thou. "Presence . . . is there only to the

extent that . . . encounter, relation, is there. Only as the Thou
becomes present does presence rise up" (*Du,* p 86). The Thou
becomes present upon the utterance of the Word: presence is
resonance. It vibrates. It flows. It moves over the face of the
deep, drawing I and Thou from either shore toward the center,
toward the vortex of the Word. What the Wandering Jew said
to Wiesel, that "God means movement and not explanation," [17] may also be said of presence.

The movement that signals the apotheosis of presence is the
movement of encounter. "All actual life is encounter," Buber
asserts (*Du,* p. 85), and all actual encounter is between I and
Thou. Let us lend an ear to Wiesel:

> If the Baal Shem could have met Rabbi Haim Ben-Atar, who was
> awaiting him in the Holy Land, together the two men would have
> hastened the coming of the Messiah, or so says Hasidic tradition,
> with the stress on encounter. Every encounter quickens the steps
> of the Redeemer; let two beings become one and the world is no
> longer the same; let two human creatures accept one another, and
> creation will have meaning, the meaning they will have imposed
> upon it. That is the new idea introduced into Jewish life by Hasi-
> dism. [*Souls,* p. 33]

And in *The Oath,* Wiesel quotes a zaddik, a holy man, saying:
"Man changes wherever he confronts his fellow man, who, in
turn, undergoes an essential change. Thus every encounter
suggests infinity. Which means: the self is linked to infinity
only through the intermediary of another self, another consciousness." [18] Here it must be pointed out that for encounter
to occur, an I must say Thou with the whole of his or her
being; and for this to occur, all the bulwarks and baggage of
ego, all the isolating marks of distinction, must be left on
shore. The Thou, both human and divine, is not above the I
but before the I. "The real heights," we read in *The Town
Beyond the Wall,* "are like the real depths: you find them at
your own level, in simple and honest conversation, in glances
heavy with existence." [19] Rebbe David of Lelov (d. 1813) once
observed in this connection that the *yud* is the smallest sign in
the Hebrew alphabet, a mere dot, but when two are placed side

by side, they signify the name of God; placed one above the
other, they indicate an interruption (*Erzählungen,* p. 570).
And interruption here is but another word for absence. As
Buber has noted, "In setting itself apart from others, the ego
removes itself from Being" (*Du,* p. 121)—and from life: the
isolation of the ego's solitude is the isolation of a tomb, where
the movement of the I degenerates into the sediment of the It.

This view of solitude is essential to Wiesel's understanding
of Hasidism; what Buber implies, Wiesel makes explicit.
"Man's role," he declares, "is to mitigate solitude; whoever
opts for solitude chooses the side of death" (*Souls,* p. 33).
And: "A Hasid alone is not a true Hasid. Solitude and Hasidism are incompatible." [20] And: "What is Hasidism if not an
attempt to tear down everything that separates one man from
another—and from himself?" (*Four,* p. 80). Here solitude
means isolation from the Word, from relation; it means stasis,
stagnation. We can think alone, but we can love only with
another. Just as presence arises in the encounter between I and
Thou, absence worms it way into a person when she isolates
herself from her Thou. It cuts a wound into the soul, cuts the
self off from itself. The man foundering in the snares of solitude, the man cut off from himself, is a man in despair, suffering from what Kierkegaard calls the sickness unto death. The
hale and whole self finds it presence only in the oneness of the
I-Thou relation. The Hasidic struggle against solitude, then, is
a struggle against despair.

Perhaps more deeply than Buber, certainly more dreadfully
than Buber, Wiesel knows what it means to empty to the bitter
dregs the cup of despair, to cry from the abyss of Night, "Eli,
Eli, lama sabachthani?" Indeed, the interest in the relation between solitude and despair—an interest that is present only by
implication in Buber's writings—is a prominent concern in
Wiesel's works, particularly in *Four Hasidic Masters* and
Somewhere a Master. In the former work the theme finds its
culmination in the fourth portrait presented, that of Rebbe
Naphtali of Ropshitz (d. 1827), a man who spent the last
months of his life in silence and seclusion:

Then came the last day. The sick father and his son are alone. "Speak, Father," begs Reb Eliezer. "Say something, one word," The old man looks at him and says nothing. "You can," pleads the son, "I know you can; you can speak. Why don't you? Why don't you want to speak, Father?"

The old Master stares at him for a long, long moment and then replies in a slow, burning whisper, "I . . . am . . . afraid. Do you . . . understand? Do you understand, Eliezer? I. Am. Afraid." [*Four*, p. 120]

The wall that isolates, the link between isolation and despair, is fear. When in the same work Wiesel reports the dread that befell Pinhas of Koretz (d. 1791), he raises the question of whether Pinhas had foreseen the end of Koretz, which occurred on Succoth, 1941 (p. 26). And in his discussion of the Great Fall of the Seer of Lublin (d. 1815)—to which Buber has been part of "a strange conspiracy of silence" (p. 64)— Wiesel asks:

Could it also be that in a sudden flash of fear the Seer had a glimpse of the distant future when night would descend upon the Jewish people and particularly upon its most compassionate and generous children—those of the Hasidic community?
. . . Lublin, during the darkest hours, became a center for torment and death. Lublin, an ingathering place for condemned Jews, led to nearby Belzec. Lublin meant Majdanek. Lublin meant that great fall not of one man, nor of one people, but of mankind. [Pp. 94–95]

There is very little intimation of such despair, of such isolation in despair, in Buber's representation of Hasidism. Buber's historical position precludes the associations Wiesel makes. From a standpoint unknown to Buber—from within the sealed trains—Wiesel insists that "Hasidism is a movement out of despair, away from despair—a movement against despair" (p. 95). And the movement away from isolation and despair is a movement toward human being, toward the Thou.

Like Wiesel, Buber knows that despair means the fragmentation and absence of self; it means the isolation of a person from her Thou and therefore from herself. The Hasidic movement against despair is a movement toward presence, toward God, toward oneself, by way of the Thou. It is the movement through which the I becomes what it is by saying Thou. Where presence is concerned, the verb is not *to be* but *to become.* "Becoming I," Buber writes, "I say Thou" (*Du,* p. 85). Saying Thou, I become present: the air vibrates with the intonation of my voice. A bridge spans a gulf and solitude is mitigated. I and Thou create a single presence, and this is the opposite of despair's isolation. In his *Célébration biblique,* or *Messengers of God,* Wiesel tells us: "In the beginning man is alone. Like God. Opening his eyes, he does not demand, 'Who am I?' but 'Who art Thou?' "[21] Adam becomes Adam by addressing God, and God is present in Adam's address. And the fact that God can be addressed makes it possible to say Thou, the word that makes all things possible. Again, on the Hasidic view, presence is the presence of God, a notion that twists and turns throughout the writings of Buber and Wiesel. God is there where I and Thou are there, gathered together in God's good name, in the name of the Nameless One who yet has a name: Thou. I argued above that the apotheosis of presence is a transformation effected by the power of the Word. What word? Thou.

The link between the power of the Word and the relation of I and Thou reveals something more about presence. Listen to Buber:

> Spirit . . . is the human being's response to his Thou. . . . Spirit is one, the response to the Thou who emerges from the mystery and addresses us from the mystery. Spirit is Word. . . . Spirit is not in the I but between I and Thou. It is not like the blood that circulates within you but like the air in which you breathe. Man lives in the Spirit when he is able to respond to his Thou. And he is able to do that whenever he enters into the relation with the whole of his being. It is only by virtue of man's power of relation that he is able to live in the Spirit. [*Du,* p. 103]

The power of the Word is the power of relation, the ability of an I to hear and respond to a Thou. Presence rises up within the relation between I and Thou; presence is Spirit, a tide that joins two shores of an abyss; it is a constant going-forth, yet it never budges from the spot. Hasidism's attempt to remove the barriers that separate I and Thou—the barriers that reduce each to an It—is an attempt to allow the Spirit to enter where it has been walled out, to breathe where it has been suffocated. As soon as the Spirit enters, it breathes life into the present moment by allowing I and Thou to breathe. This movement of breathing life into the moment is the movement by which presence is transformed, apotheosized; for God is Spirit. "God dwells," said Menahem Mendl of Kotzk (d. 1859), "where He is allowed to enter" (*Erzählungen*, p. 664; see also *Mendiant*, p. 147). He enters through the portal of the Word by which the I says Thou and life is breathed into both—by which the I says Thou with his whole being and thus becomes one with that Word.

To say Thou in such a manner is to say Thou lovingly, joyously, gratefully—in short, passionately. If the Spirit enters where the barriers have been removed, it is passion that removes them. The eruption of the Word, the pulsation of encounter, the tide of transformation—all such movement is the movement of passion.

The Movement of Passion

"I have no use for curiosity," affirms a beggar in *Le mendiant de Jérusalem*. "Passion alone attracts me" (p. 166). Passion: this is where the distinction between Buber and Wiesel is most pronounced. Again, while Buber structures Hasidism by giving equal measure to *hitlahavut, avoda, kavanna,* and *shiflut,* Wiesel places the accent on *hitlahavut,* on the soul aflame with passion. Indeed, he is himself a soul on fire; it has been said that to read Wiesel is to burn with him. And so it is. He who has seen so many consumed in the flames of death now struggles to kindle the fire of life. He who has seen philosophy itself reduced to ashes now turns to the tale to stir the embers.

In his treatment of the Holy Seer of Lublin, for instance, Wiesel writes:

The Seer advocated passion and compassion, and enthusiasm, fervor—*hitlahavut*—fervor above all. "I prefer an opponent—a passionate Mitnagged—rather than a lukewarm Hasid," he said. For absence of fire, absence of passion, leads to indifference and resignation—in other words, to death. What is worse than suffering? Indifference. What is worse than despair? Resignation—the inability to be moved, to let oneself go, to let one's imagination catch fire. [*Four*, p. 81]

Much more so than Buber, Wiesel casts Hasidism in terms of a struggle against indifference. While Buber renounced the indifference of the mystic and then went on, Wiesel sustains the attack on indifference, on an indifference even more deadly than that of the mystic: the indifference of the spectator. In *The Town Beyond the Wall*, for example, we read:

The spectator has nothing of the human in him: he is a stone in the street, the cadaver of an animal, a pile of dead wood. He is there, he survives us, he is immobile. The spectator reduces himself to the level of an object. He is no longer he, you, or I: he is "it." [P. 171]

If all actual life is encounter, all death is the absence of encounter. We flee from the Word to the comfort of idle talk, from relation to separation; we construct walls of convenience and convention to hide from the hand that reaches out to us, from the voice that beckons us; we cling to the calm and security of the It rather than turn ourselves over to the fire and the whirlwind of the Thou. But the walls within which we inter ourselves are the walls of a tomb. As Wiesel sees it, the spectator is one of those "who are dead and do not know it" (*Oath*, p. 196). His ears are the ears of a wall, his tongue the tongue of a stone.

From the standpoint of Word and Spirit, to bring to life is to call into presence by virtue of passion. An I responds to a Thou, and a wound is healed: in this way passion makes whole the man who has suffered the sickness unto death. This is the Spirit's movement at the spot, its going forth without budging from the spot, rather like a dance. To be sure, the purest form of *hitlahavut*, as Buber observes, is the dance (*Leben*, pp. 23–

24). And Wiesel reports that Rebbe Leib, the first rebbe to turn dance into a ritual, was told by the son of the Maggid of Mezeritch, "Your dancing counts for more than my prayers" (*Souls*, p. 46). For the Hasid's dance is a dance of joy, a leap into the heavens, a defiance of gravity. It can open gates that are impervious to prayer; it can gather eternity into the present and the dancer into the dance. As Buber expresses it, in the passion of *hitlahavut*, "all that lies in the past, all that lies in the future, is gathered together in the present. Time shrinks, the line between eternities disappears; only the moment lives, and the moment is eternity" (*Leben*, p. 23). The dance of joy is the dance of eternity in time; it is the dance of presence. Eternity has entered the moment because the dance of joy—when it has no ground other than itself—draws possibility into the moment. The dance declares that joy and passion need no ground; the chain of cause and effect is the force of gravity that the dance overcomes. When that chain is broken, eternity has room to enter time—or to displace it—as reality takes over illusion. For according to Nahman of Bratzlav, time does not exist (*Souls*, p. 181).

We have seen that Wiesel, more persistently than Buber, penetrates the substance of Hasidism as a movement away from despair. Likewise, more insistently than Buber, Wiesel brings out the significance of Hasidism as a resounding call to joy. Why joy? Because, Wiesel says, quoting the Baal Shem:

> "The man who looks only at himself cannot but sink into despair, yet as soon as he opens his eyes to the creation around him, he will know joy." And this joy leads to the absolute, to redemption, to God; that was the new truth as defined by the Baal Shem. [*Souls*, p. 26]

The call to joy is a call to presence, to the divinity of presence. For "God dwells in joy," declares Wiesel. "God is joy, God is song and fervor" (*Generation*, p. 219). The Hasidic summons to passionate, flaming joy is itself a song of joy. It is the joy in joy that Bergson describes as life's attachment to life, which was discussed in chapter 1. Listen: "What is a Hasid? Someone who possesses a precious key, a key that opens all the

doors, even those that God keeps closed. And the key is . . .
the *Nigoun,* the song of joy that makes our hearts thrill. The
Nigoun opens the gates of heaven. Melancholy closes them"
(*Four,* p. 117). The key that opens all the doors is the key to
presence: presence is the Open, the openness of a heart rapt
with passion. While the scholars had thought to open the gates
with the keys of the Commandments, the Hasidim discovered
that each person holds the key within. The scholar stands before the Law, but the Hasid moves within the song; present in
the song of joy, the Hasid is presence itself.

The relation of I and Thou runs deepest, the power of the
Word is greatest, in the song and dance of joy. And the joy is
most passionate when the vault of the Night would suffocate
it, when by all that is conceivable it should be dead. Again, in
his collision with the Night, Wiesel fathoms unpenetrated
depths of Hasidism. Says his rebbe in *The Gates of the Forest:*

> The man who goes singing to death is the brother of the man who
> goes to death fighting. . . . Do you know what that song hides?
> A dagger, an outcry. . . . There is joy as well as fury in the *ha-
> sid's* dancing. It is a way of proclaiming, "You don't want me to
> dance; too bad, I'll dance anyhow. You've taken away every rea-
> son for singing, but I shall sing. . . . You didn't expect my joy,
> but here it is; yes, my joy will rise up." [P. 198]

This is joy at the edge of the abyss, a joy that rises from the
depths, a joy that is itself a deep that calls unto deep. It is at
once a beckoning and a response. In this case, it will be noted,
there is an element of defiance in joy, an insistence on affirming life when the temptation to despair is greatest. If despair
isolates a man from himself, joy makes him whole, at one with
himself. And he who is whole is wholly present. Joy's connection with presence lies in the wholeness it brings, which is
necessary to presence: genuine presence is joyful presence.

Joy that has no reasonable ground is a joy steeped in passion, and this passion has a name: love. He who cannot rejoice
cannot love; he who cannot love cannot rejoice. The presence
that arises between I and Thou is the presence of love. Thus
Buber tells us that a fundamental watchword of Hasidism is to

love more (*Leben,* p. 43). And Wiesel points out that "Hasidism defined itself, and its relation to its members, in terms of love—exclusively" (*Somewhere,* p. 39). Nor should love here be confused with feelings. In *Ich und Du,* Buber explains "We 'have' feelings, but love is an event. Feelings reside in man, but man dwells in his love. . . . Love does not cling to an I, as if the Thou were its 'content' or object; it is *between* I and Thou" (*Du,* p. 87). And this means that love is God; everywhere Buber uses the term *love* he could substitute the word *presence:* presence is an event, the event of dwelling in a relationship of love. If the passion of love burns within, it dwells equally in the Open; in love it is the soul that envelops the body.

Presence teems in the polarty between I and Thou, and it is love that makes presence vibrate with apotheosis: God is love. God is present where God is loved, and God is loved where man is loved. This is what the Baal Shem imparted to the Hasidim: he who loves, loves God (*Souls,* p. 31). To study the Law and keep the Commandments is all very good, but without love all remains to be done. If, as Buber has asserted, Hasidism is a mysticism that hallows time (*Botschaft,* p. 894), it does so through love. A moment filled with the *hitlahavut* of love is a moment filled—and thus fulfilled—with the eternal; the kingdom draws nigh, and the gates of heaven open. Again, recall the words of the Baal Shem: "If I love God, what need have I of a world to come?" Where love is present, where the eternal has entered the moment, there lies the world to come; the gates that are open are gates forever before us.

In Wiesel's *The Trial of God,* a young woman named Hanna informs the other characters that she hears voices; when asked what they say, she replies: "They say that love is possible. And pleasant. That happiness is God's gift to all of His children. They tell me: 'Dance.' And I dance. They tell me: 'Sing.' And I dance and sing. They tell me: 'Love.' And I love. . . . They tell me: 'Live.' " [22] The first three imperatives amount to the fourth; there is but a single message: be present. How? Love. The tales of the Hasidim abound in the passionate emphasis on love. When a father came to the Baal Shem, for example,

and asked what to do about his son's straying from God, the
master replied, "Love him more" (*Leben*, p. 43). The dis-
ciples of Pinhas of Koretz taught: "When you find that someone hates you and does you harm, you must love him more than
before" (*Erzählungen*, p. 248). Rebbe Shmelke of Nikolsburg
(d. 1778) interpreted "My enemy will not triumph over me"
(Ps. 41:11) to mean "My enemy will suffer no harm because
of me" (*Erzählungen*, p. 308). And Aharon of Karlin once
said that if Hasidim meet and have no story or song to share,
then they should share their love; says Wiesel, "This advice—
more than any other saying uttered by any Master—summa-
rizes the attitude of the Hasidic movement" (*Somewhere*,
pp. 29–30).

Like the song and dance of the Hasidim, love is most passionate, most genuine, when it has the least to support it.
There is no reason to love those who have harmed us, no basis
for loving the man who has turned his back on God. This is
why there is more of the interrogative than the declarative
about love and the passion with which it burns. In *The Accident*, Wiesel writes, "Love is a question mark, not an exclamation point."[23] And in *Five Biblical Portraits*, he asserts,
"Most good questions remain questions";[24] so it is with love.
Like the word *love*, the word *question* is both noun and verb,
and the two forms of the word intersect in presence. Here we
find another point that distinguishes Buber from Wiesel. The
fuel that stokes the fire of a man's passion? The force that sets
him in motion? His love, his question. An insight: "The Jew
is in perpetual motion. He is characterized as much by his
quest as by his faith. . . . He defines himself more by what
troubles him than by what reassures him. . . . To me, the Jew
and his questioning are one" (*Generation*, p. 214). And a
prayer: "I no longer ask You to resolve my questions, only to
receive them and make them part of You" (p. 241). Unlike
Buber, Wiesel has seen that a person's question is essential to
the movement of his passion, to the relation to his Thou, to
the Word he voices or holds back—in short, question is essential to presence. In order to say, "Here I am," we must first be
able to ask, "Where am I?"—and, "Why am I here?"

Presence rises up where questions are raised, and such questions are raised in the movement of passion. The power of the Word is the passion of the Word, and the relation between I and Thou lies in the passion between I and Thou, in the questions by which one addresses the other. In Hasidism the questions take the form of tales and legends. Here the summons is more vital than the teaching, the response more needful than the learning. What Wiesel has said of the Holy Seer of Lublin may be said of Hasidism in general: "He taught his followers not how to study but how to listen, how to share, how to feel, how to pray, how to laugh, how to hope—how to live" (*Four*, p. 88). And to live is to be present.

Conclusion

Rabbi Yitzhak of Vorki (d. 1848) once asserted that Adam's real sin lay in his anxiety over the next day (*Erzählungen*, p. 681), that is, in his removal from presence. Reflecting a similar line of thought, Buber, in *Das Problem des Menschen* (*The Problem of Man*), makes the following statement, in words that bear the imprint of his Hasidic roots:

> If I am not actually here, I am guilty. If I answer the call of present being—"Where art thou?"—with "Here I am," but am not actually here, that is, not with the truth of my whole being, then I am guilty. The primal condition of guilt lies in remaining-within-oneself. If a form and appearance of present being should move past me and I am not actually here, then out of the distance of its fading comes a second call, so softly and secretly that it might have come from myself: "Where were you?" [25]

To respond "with the truth of my whole being" is to respond joyfully, lovingly, gratefully—with all the ingredients of faith. Only the person who is wholly and passionately engaged in the relation and the response to her Thou can reply, "Here I am," when called. He who is isolated within himself is isolated *from* himself and therefore from presence. What is sin? On the Hasidic view, "sin is that which, by its nature, cannot be done with the whole being" (*Botschaft*, p. 802). The state of sin, in other words, is a state of absence, the sickness unto death. Presence, with the life that cuts through it, is a state of grace, and herein lies its apotheosis.

Presence is much like a child, and like no adult, the child knows how to be present, free of the masks of calculation and pretense that haunt the fallen man. Looking once again at Buber's philosophical insight, we see that he has more than an inkling of the relation between child and presence: "This indomitably flowing potentiality is the reality 'child.' This emergence of singularity, which is more than mere birth and begetting, this grace of beginning again and ever again" (*Erziehung,* p. 787). Bearing in mind that this comes from Buber's *Reden über Erziehung* (*Discourses on Education*), we would do well to recall that the seeds of Hasidism were planted when the young Baal Shem led the children to their studies in a procession of song. Hasidism rises up neither in tract nor in treatise but in the song of a child: it begins with the grace of beginning again and ever again.

If Hasidism begins among children, the role of the child in Wiesel's literature—much more so than in Buber's philosophy—provides us with an indication of where Hasidism may stand today. For example, consider—as dreadful as it is to repeat—the following scene from *Night,* in which the hanging of a child is described:

> For more than half an hour he stayed there, struggling between life and death, dying in slow agony under our eyes. . . . He was still alive when I passed in front of him. His tongue was still red, his eyes not yet glazed.
>   Behind me, I heard the same man asking:
>   "Where is God now?"
>   And I heard a voice within me answer him:
>   "Where is He? Here He is—He is hanging here on these gallows." [26]

And in *Le mendiant de Jérusalem* we read, if we dare read further,

> The death of a man is only the death of a man, while the death of a child is the death of innocence, the death of God in the heart of

man. And he who does not drink deeply of this truth, who does not then shout it from the rooftops, is a man void of heart and of God, a man who has never seen the misty eyes of a child who has passed away without a moan, who has died to show his parents the way and to reveal the path that awaits them. [P. 91]

This is where the path of Hasidism—after a descent into the pit of Night—has led Wiesel. Again, for Buber the Hasidic apotheosis of presence means recognizing God *in* the moment, while for Wiesel it means resurrecting God *to* the moment. This is where the power of the Word, the relation of I and Thou, and the movement of passion converge, and Wiesel struggles to make them converge not through philosophical manifesto but through the echo of the tales and legends of which Hasidism itself is made. Whereas the philosopher had examined an existing Hasidic kingdom, the novelist found that he had to regenerate a kingdom that had been reduced to ashes. And this he has done by breathing the literary Word into those ashes.

PART THREE

Messianic Elements of Language and Literature

AT THIS POINT we begin a movement of return within the parameters of this book. Setting out from the Johannine logos, we have traced a few strands of connection running through religion, language, and literature. If we can regard the Johannine logos in terms of a concept that views the Messiah as Word, then it is appropriate that in the third, and last, part of this volume we examine the messianic elements of language and literature. Although Saint John and Elie Wiesel differ in that one is Christian and the other is not, they have something in common in that they belong to a tradition of messianism and that they associate the Word with messianism. In this book we began with religion; we now end with literature. Yet in the cycles of relations that bind religion, language, and literature, we might have begun and ended with any of the three. And the movement along the avenues of those relations is always a movement of return.

Where do we return? To life. Throughout this book we have viewed religion from the perspective of life's attachment to life. When that attachment is lost, we are fallen; when it is regained, we are redeemed. And that which makes such redemption possible is messianic in essence. Chapter 7, "Messianic Aspects of the Child in the Works of Elie Wiesel," examines a literary treatment of one means of redemption and return to life. It deals with a number of works and with some general features of the messianic elements of language and literature. Chapter 8, on Wiesel's *The Testament,* however, discusses specific elements of language and literature that have messianic characteristics, using the preceding chapter as background. The chapters in part three combine to speak what has been spoken between the lines in part one and part two, namely that literature and our relation to it constitute an effort to regain a religious presence in life through the Word. And because literature and the literary Word define that effort, they harbor the echo of that name in search of being which is the Messiah.

CHAPTER SEVEN

Messianic Aspects of the Child in the Works of Elie Wiesel

IN THE JUDEO-CHRISTIAN tradition the Messiah is the one who leads the exiled to the kingdom, the banished to the garden, the fallen to redemption. He is the one who is awaited and is yet among us, the one who is before Abraham was. He is the child who shows us how to become as a child after we have squandered our souls in a vain effort to become as the gods. For it will be recalled that in both testaments of the Bible, the Messiah is associated with the child. Isaiah proclaims, for example, that "the wolf shall dwell with the lamb, and the leopard shall lie down with the kid. . . . And a little child shall lead them" (Isa. 11:6). And in the New Testament we read, "This shall be a sign unto you: you will find a babe . . . lying in a manger" (Luke 2:12), where the sign of the child, and not the manger, signals the coming of the Messiah.

A glance through the annals of the Western world literature will show that the Messiah is among the principle concerns of many and varied authors, from Dante to Kazantzakis, from Milton to Dostoevsky. Like many before him, Elie Wiesel devotes much of his art to the Messiah. Unlike most before him, however, Wiesel explores the definitive connection between child and Messiah. And unlike anyone before him, he pursues this link by the light of the flames that consumed a generation of children: he struggles with the messianic aspects of the child along the edges of the Night that swallowed up Judeo-Christian tradition and transformed every notion of innocence, of God, of meaning. Such a transformation cannot occur without changing the ways in which we ponder the relation between child and Messiah.

Commenting on the Nazis' extermination of the children, Wiesel writes: "It is as though the Nazi killers knew precisely what children represent to us. According to our tradition, the entire world subsists thanks to them." [1] Since the world is made of living individuals, each individual lives by the grace of the children: in them dwells our Savior and Redeemer. But what becomes of our redemption when the children are reduced to ashes by the hands of those whom they redeem? What happens to the relation between child and Messiah? And to the relation between man and himself? Examining the messianic aspects of the child in Wiesel's works may help us find the answers to these questions; or, failing that, perhaps Wiesel can show us how to sustain them, show us the courage to live with them, so that the questions themselves may become part of the messianic essence of the child. Let us, then, gather ourselves and explore Wiesel's portrayal of the child as victim, as savior, and as an integral part of man's relation to himself. For these are the pathways along which child and Messiah meet in the works of Elie Wiesel.

The Child as Victim

In Wiesel's novel *The Oath,* Moshe declares: "We seek the Messiah. We pursue him. We think he is in heaven; we don't know that he likes to come down as a child. Except that today it has become a game to kill childhood." [2] And on the day we play that game we surely die. The Messiah may indeed walk among us in the guise of a child, but the quest for the Messiah arises only in the aftermath of the murder of the child. Only the dead seek life, and the real death is the death of the child: like Adam standing over the body of Abel, the man who cries out for the Messiah is a man standing over the body of a child. To be a child is to be a victim; to be a man is to be a survivor. Each is separated from the other by an abyss: as Wiesel has said, at such moments of death the earth does indeed gape, and we plunge headlong into the void.[3] The bulwarks around us and the ground beneath us crumble; the ready-made truths that once provided meaning and direction perish.

The death of the child, then, is always the death of something more. As Michael in *The Town beyond the Wall* says, "A child who dies becomes the center of the universe: stars and meadows die with him" (p. 99). Looking further at the death of the child Yankel in that novel, we read, "The earth had tilted on its axis, and the sun had ceased to govern it" (p. 100). Where there had been a child, we now encounter a gaping black hole; where there had been a world, we now discover a wasteland. But there is more still. How much more is revealed in the following lines from Wiesel's *Night*, certainly among the most dreadful in all literature. A portion of the passage was introduced in the last chapter; we now plunge deeper into it:

> One day when we came back from work, we saw three gallows rearing up in the assembly place. . . . Roll call. SS all around us, machine guns trained: the traditional ceremony. Three victims in chains—and one of them, the little servant, the sad-eyed angel.
>
> The SS seemed more preoccupied, more disturbed than usual. To hang a young boy on front of thousands of spectators was no light matter. . . . All eyes were on the child. He was lividly pale, almost calm, biting his lips. The gallows threw its shadow over him. . . .
>
> "Where is God? Where is He?" someone behind me asked.
>
> At a sign from the head of the camp, the three chairs tipped over. . . .
>
> The third rope was still moving; being so light, the child was still alive.
>
> For more than half an hour he stayed there, struggling between life and death, dying in slow agony under our eyes. . . .
>
> Behind me, I heard the same man asking: "Where is God now?"
>
> And I heard a voice within me answer him: "Where is He? Here He is—He is hanging here on these gallows."[4]

In this passage from Wiesel's one work dealing with his camp experiences, a witness emerges to make witnesses of us all.

Though it is only the sixth hour, darkness descends over the face of the earth, the darkness of the death of God. Wiesel went to the camps as a child of fifteen, and the child who witnesses the death of God witnesses the death of himself as a child. The sun turns to darkness and the moon turns to blood; the light that had guided him is extinguished. This is the fall, the collision with nothingness, that initiates Wiesel's search for the child and for the resurrection of the child.

For Michael in *The Town Beyond the Wall*, the search for the victimized child takes the form of a pursuit of God, not so much to find and embrace him as to demand an explanation from him. "I'll follow Him everywhere," he insists, "in time and in the universe. He won't get away; I'll stay on His trail whatever happens, whether He likes it or not. He took my childhood; I have a right to ask Him what He did with it" (p. 59). Michael seeks a reckoning from God because God is to be found in the executioner as well as in the victim; his is the hand that strikes the blow, his the hand that pleads for mercy. But, we must ask, who indeed is the executioner when the child within is the victim? There is a passage in Wiesel's *One Generation After* that may help in this regard. It consists of a dialogue between Wiesel and the Other—perhaps the Angel of Death, perhaps God, perhaps both. The Other speaks first:

> *Don't touch the mirror; it might break. And I cannot do without it; I need it, do you hear me, I need it!*
> Don't worry. I won't be the one to break your mirror: the child will. And you are powerless against him. And he's not trembling. He is dead. You permitted him to escape your grasp.
> *It's incredible: you refuse to understand. I wasn't the one who killed him. It was you.*[5]

Here it looks as though the child within dies by suicide. He sees his image in the mirror, but the hour comes, the sixth hour, when the mirror rejects him, and with his own hand he breaks the glass. And once this occurs, the hand raised against the child in the mirror may be directed against the child before us. Like the first death, the death of the child is always a murder, a homicide—and a suicide—by which we kill what resembles us.

Thus, like Cain, the killer is led to kill, to return to chaos a universe that has turned to chaos; like Cain, he kills to become God—and to kill God.[6] As Wiesel states in *Le mendiant de Jérusalem:* "He who kills becomes God. He who kills kills God. Every murder is a suicide in which the Eternal is eternally the victim."[7] If the Messiah is the God-man, the murderer is the man-god, the man who usurps the throne of a dead God. Here one catches a glimpse of the bond between the executioner and the victim: the executioner is a murdered child bent on murdering the child, a man to whom redemption has been denied and who therefore sets out to destroy every trace of the Redeemer. This is the event that Eliezer witnessed when the "sad little angel" was murdered on the gallows of Buna. Witnessing the execution of the child, he witnessed not only the death of God but the death of the Redeemer. And so he fell. Like the five-year-old Joel in *A Jew Today,* he "was left alone in the darkness. His hand covering his mouth, he began to sob without a sound, scream without a sound, survive without a sound" (p. 132).

Keeping this image before us, let us dare to look upon another victim described in *A Jew Today;* both are engulfed by the Night, and the silence of the one permeates the words of the other.

> She was six years old, a pale, shy and nervous child. Did she know what was happening around her? . . . She saw the killers, she saw them kill—how did she translate these visions in her child's mind?
>
> One morning she asked her mother to hug her. Then she came to place a kiss on her father's forehead. And she said, "I think that I shall die today." And after a sigh, a long sigh: "I think I am glad."
>
> Thus my friend Shimshon learned that his little girl knew more about life and the meaning of life than many old people. [P. 128]

Both through Joel and through the little girl, one encounters, in fear and trembling, the child as victim. With the child, everything has meaning and all things are possible; without the child, no dawn can penetrate the Night, and the only reality is death: "I think that I shall die today. I think I am glad." The wisdom imparted to Shimshon? That when life makes a child glad to die, life itself is but a living death; that the lamb cannot dwell with the wolf nor the kid lie down with the leopard without being devoured; and that there is no child to lead them. Shimshon learned what Wiesel learned; like Shimshon, Wiesel was educated by the flames that swallowed up the soul and support of the world. In *Ani Maamin,* he cries:

> With each hour, the most blessed and most stricken people of the world number twelve times twelve children less. And each one carries away still another fragment of the Temple in flames. Flames—never before have there been such flames. And in every one of them it is the vision of the Redeemer that is dying.[8]

The dead child is the dead Messiah: the Messiah is the victim.

Again, the survivor is the man who has survived the death of the child. Whether the child is within him or before him, the death is one; it is shrouded with the same silence, haunted by the same need for redemption. Because the passing of the child generates the need for redemption, the silence that goes with death brings with it a kind of judgment, a Last Judgment, in which the survivor comes before himself and his own silence. Let us listen to the voice of a victimized child who speaks for all the victims; it comes from Wiesel's *Dawn:*

> We're not here to sit in judgment. We're here simply because you're here. We're present wherever you go; we are what you do. When you raise your eyes to Heaven, we share in their sight; when you pat the head of a hungry child a thousand hands are laid on his head; when you give bread to a beggar we give him that taste of paradise which only the poor can savor. Why are we silent? Because silence is not only our dwelling place but our very being as well. We *are* silence. And your silence is us. You carry us with you. . . . When you see us you imagine that we are sitting in judgment on you. You are wrong. Your silence is your judge.[9]

Here the voice of the victim rings like the voice of the Paraclete, of the Comforter, whom we seek and who is yet among us as long as there is a child among us. For the child opens the way to the one we have lost, to the one we have murdered. The one path to redemption leads to the child; or better, the child *is* the path, is the way to a resurrection from the ashes and a reaffirmation of life. The victim is the savior.

The Child as Savior

To begin this section, a passage from *Le mendiant de Jérusalem,* cited in the last chapter, should be recalled:

> The death of a man is only the death of a man, while the death of a child is the death of innocence, the death of God in the heart of man. And he who does not drink deeply of this truth, who does not then shout it from the rooftops, is a man void of heart and of God, a man who has never seen the misty eyes of a child who has passed away without a moan, who has died to show his parents the way and to reveal the path that awaits them. [P. 91]

If the real death is the death of the child, the real revelation is the one couched in the little one's death. The child's death reveals something to the adult that can be revealed in no other way; it unveils for the adult a truth that can be found in no other way; and it offers the adult a salvation that can be had in no other way. In short, the child dies for the man; becoming the victim, he becomes the savior. Each time a little one dies, God offers his only begotten child so that the fallen might be saved.

In *The Testament,* Wiesel provides us with an image of a fallen man for whom a little one dies. The scene is an East European battlefield during the Second World War; the speaker is Paltiel Kossover, a medic in the Red Army and the main character in the novel. Describing a young, wounded soldier, Paltiel says:

> He was beautiful and light as a child. I spoke to him as I always did, repeating what I always said to my dead: "Don't worry, my little one, we are almost there."
> . . . My guardian angel on my shoulders, I moved forward, tripping. Then I was lifted off the ground. Violent red pain. I

opened my eyes: the impact had thrown me into a trench. Torn to
bits, he was nothing but a decapitated, legless corpse. He had
saved my life: I was only wounded.[10]

We think we save the child. Not a bit of it. The child saves
us. How? By offering us the chance to save him. Although
Paltiel's "guardian angel" is a soldier in the Russian army, it
will be observed that Paltiel compares him to a child and addresses him as a child. One should also note the echoes of a
fall in the passage above: Paltiel trips before he is saved and
then lives to rise from the trench like a man rising from the
grave. The literal fragmentation of the child should be pointed
out too; the fate of the child who dies in the place of the man
graphically reflects the fragmentation of the soul that characterizes the fallen man.

The fallen man is the man within whom the child has died,
the man who is no longer as a child; yet it is the child who he
no longer is that must save him. In *The Gates of the Forest,*
for example, a child ultimately leads the main character, Gregor,
back to himself as a child, to himself as Gavriel, the name
given to him as a child; the name bears the child, and the
name of the child opens the path to redemption. Redemption
in this case cannot come from God; it can come only from the
child within, the child who the man once was and whom he
has allowed to die. In this connection we find a prayer uttered
in *One Generation After,* a prayer that is as disturbing as it is
revealing:

> I ask You, God of Abraham, Isaac and Jacob, to enable me to
> pronounce these words without betraying the child that transmit-
> ted them to me: God of Abraham, Isaac and Jacob, enable me to
> forgive You and enable the child I once was to forgive me too.
>   I no longer ask You for the life of that child, nor even for his
> faith. I only beg You to listen to him and act in such a way that
> You and I can listen to him together. [P. 242]

These lines are revealing because they point up a link between
salvation and forgiveness: if the child is the savior, it is because he is the source of forgiveness. These words, however,

also bear the disturbing implication that God himself is in need of forgiveness, that the child may bring redemption even to God. In this regard Wiesel teaches us something more about the messianic elements of the child. The child who appears as the savior of man is the child who God becomes in order to redeem himself. "These children," Abraham cries in *Ani Maamin,* "have taken Your countenance, O God" (p. 57). The Messiah is the God who, out of love for man, has renounced his godhead to become a child. Thus messianism transforms both God and man. Who works this transformation? A little child.

As a savior, then, the child draws God and human being closer together; again, the child is the God-man, the one who mitigates the solitude of each. "In the beginning," Wiesel asserts in *Célébration biblique,* "man is alone. Like God" (p. 15). And in *The Oath* Moshe says: "What is the Messiah . . . if not man transcending his solitude in order to make his fellow man less solitary? To turn a single human being back toward life is to prevent the destruction of the world, says the Talmud" (pp. 90–91). These lines reveal another facet of the messianic aspects of the child. The child born to us is the one who makes our lives less solitary; teeming with the freshness and fervor of creation, he turns us back toward life's freshness and fervor. Further, if the child whom Isaiah dubbed the Prince of Peace (Isa. 9:6) comes to save the world from destruction, he does so not by saving humankind but by returning a single human being to life. For "the world was created for a single man," Wiesel writes in *Célébration biblique.* "Whoever kills a human being destroys all of humanity; whoever saves a human being saves all of humanity" (p. 20). This is what makes the relation to the child as Messiah a personal relation; or rather, the relation is a personal one because the child is the Messiah. Like death, salvation has nothing to do with the crowd; it concerns only the individual and his relation to a Thou.

Such a relation is rendered quite eloquently in *Ani Maamin,* where we find Abraham struggling to save a child:

I run
As far as my legs will carry me,
Like the wind,
With the wind,
Farther than the wind.
And while I run,
I am thinking:
This is insane,
This Jewish child
Will not be spared.
I run and run
And cry.
And while I am crying,
While I am running,
I perceive a whisper:
I believe,
Says the little girl,
Weakly,
I believe in you. [Pp. 89,91]

The return to life is a return to faith; the child's faith returns
the man to life. Yet if a child's faith can return the man to life,
so can the child's cry. Consider the following lines from *Somewhere a Master:*

Here is what happened one Yom Kippur eve:
The House of Study was packed with worshippers ready to intone the solemn and awe-inspiring prayer of Kol Nidre, but the
Rebbe was late. Where, but where could he be? What could be
more important than to lead the holy community of Sassov into
prayer—the most magnificent prayer of all? . . . Minutes went
by, long endless minutes. . . . Soon time for this prayer would be
over; it would be too late.
There was a woman among the worshippers who was worried
about her infant: she had left him home all alone, thinking she
would be back in an hour. . . . So she decided not to wait but to
go home to her child.
To her surprise she found that her infant was not alone. A man
was cradling her child, singing to him softly. Said the Rebbe,
"What could I do? As I walked past your house I heard a child
crying—I had to stay with him." [11]

What could be more important than the Kol Nidre, the prayer of atonement? Rebbe Moshe Leib of Sassov knew. And, on the eve of the Day of Atonement, he knew where his atonement lay. His cradling of the child is his embrace of life, the embrace that instills him with life and binds him to life.

In *The Testament* there is another example of a single child linking a single man to life. "Let us not speak of Raissa," Paltiel writes about his wife from his prison cell. "She is not the one who binds me to life; it is my son Grisha" (p. 147). Elsewhere in the novel there is a more striking image of the bond between Paltiel and his infant son: "The next day I put on the phylacteries again. This time I waited until Grisha woke up. He pulled at the straps, and that filled me with joy" (p. 332). Phylacteries are donned for morning prayer; they signify a union—or a communion—with God. In this scene they form a physical link between man and child; joined to the child, man is joined to God. And the sign of his relation to God is the joy that fills him. On Wiesel's view: "God dwells only in joy. God is joy, God is song and fervor" (*Generation*, p. 219). The child saves the man, then, by restoring in him the presence of God, by filling him with a joy steeped in love, and by showing him how, like the child Isaac, to transform suffering "into prayer and love rather than rancor and malediction" (*Célébration*, p. 88). This joy heals the soul afflicted with despair and makes whole the man suffering from the fragmentation of the fall. For the child's wholeness shows us how to become whole; the child's joy shows us how to rejoice; and the child's love shows us how to love.

But from the standpoint of Elie Wiesel, of one who has emerged from the depths of the sealed trains, the child opens up to us another path to salvation: it is the way of a certain madness, a messianic madness. Noted earlier was Wiesel's observation that according to Jewish tradition "the entire world subsists" thanks to the children; here one may recall the remark made by Gregor's grandfather in *The Gates of the Forest:* "Madmen are just wandering messengers, and without them the world couldn't endure." [12] The madness that saves and sustains the world is the madness of the child—or of the man who remains a child. Wiesel's play *Zalmen, or The Madness of God* revolves around one such figure. In the opening scene, Zalmen proclaims: "Never mind if I am a child. I'll probably always be one,"[13] thus establishing his presence as a child figure. In the middle of the drama—at its heart, so to speak— Zalmen reveals something about the nature of messianic madness: "One has to be mad today to believe in God and man— one has to be mad to believe. One has to be mad to remain human" (p. 79). This is the madness to be reaped from the child, the madness by which the child offers us salvation in the wake of the madness of God. What is the madness of God? Wiesel tells us in *Legends of Our Time:*

> Auschwitz signifies not only the failure of two thousand years of Christian civilization, but also the defeat of the intellect that wants to find a Meaning—with a capital *M*—in history. . . . At Auschwitz the sacrifices were without point, without faith, without divine inspiration. If the suffering of one human being has any meaning, that of six million has none. Numbers have their own importance; they prove, according to Piotr Rawicz, that God has gone mad.[14]

As a child figure in the drama, then, Zalmen takes on not the madness of God, as one might have thought, but the madness of the child who returns to God a madness of his own; if Zalmen's *is* the madness of God, it is of a God who is mad enough to become a child. Just as the child may bring salvation to the man, Zalmen brings madness to the rabbi of a synagogue in Soviet Russia at Kol Nidre. When he rises to give voice to the prayer, the rabbi shouts the agony of a man witnessing the demise of the faith and the death of God, a man faced with being "the last teacher, the last messenger, the last believer" (p. 107). The rabbi describes his moment of madness as a moment "of falling . . . upwards. A strange moment of dizziness" (p. 88); if the fall occurs in a swoon, as Kierkegaard has said, so does redemption. But whose madness was it? Was it born of the man or of the child? Zalmen lets us know at the end of the play:

At *Kol Nidre* everybody thought they were hearing the Rabbi! Zalmen was the Rabbi and the Rabbi was hiding behind Zalmen! Zalmen, the defender of his people—the soul of their silence, the silence of their hope, the dream of their dreams—he was lighting the fire and the fire did not consume him. [P. 161]

This interrelation, this interchange of identity, is essential to the event of salvation. We have seen that when a child dies, the child within dies. A chasm cuts through the man, severing him from God, from life, from himself: the fall is a fall into separation. Salvation, then, comes in a resurrection of relation, of the presence of the child within the man, whether in the form of joy and fervor or in the form of a madness that enables us to remain human. The child who redeems the man thus returns the man to a relation with himself, the relation that makes him human, whole, and hale.

The Child Within Man's Relation to Himself

In *A Jew Today,* Wiesel comments on the scrolls of the Torah, declaring that it is "impossible to unroll them without trembling; impossible to read them without becoming a child again" (p. 74). Coming before the Word of God, we come before God; coming before God, we come before the child in whom God lives; coming before the child, we come before ourselves as a child. God, Messiah, man—all are gathered together in the child. Hence, a human being's relation to God and Messiah rests on his relation to the child; and his relation to the child is the one thing needful in his relation to himself.

One example of this idea appears in *The Town Beyond the Wall,* the tale of a young man named Michael and his struggle to return to himself. Michael's closest and wisest friend is a man named Pedro. On the morning after Michael has offered his friend the most intimate details of his childhood, Pedro remarks: "I won't forget last night. From now on you can say 'I am Pedro,' and I, 'I am Michael'" (p. 131). As in the case of Wiesel himself, Michael's childhood was consumed in the flames of the Holocaust. Part of his effort to reestablish his self-identity is the attempt to resurrect the child within; another part of his endeavor lies in his saying Thou to his friend with his whole being. Elsewhere Wiesel writes, "The Messiah is that which makes man more human, which . . . stretches his soul toward others" (*Gates,* p. 33); and recall Moshe's statement in *The Oath* that the Messiah is man's transcendence of "his solitude in order to make his fellow man less solitary" (pp. 90–91). In the light of these thoughts, the messianic aspect of the child in Michael's relation to Pedro becomes more clear. The emergence of a single I-Thou presence between Michael and Pedro occurs precisely because the child has entered into the relation: Michael's relation to Pedro as a Thou is rooted in his relation to the child within. And both contribute to his relation to himself. Who is the child? The child is Thou.

Not long after this interchange of identity between Michael and Pedro, a telling prayer flashes through Michael's mind: "God of my childhood, show me the way that leads to myself" (p. 136). The God of childhood is the God of the child, the God who abides in the child. Central to Michael's effort to become himself is his compulsion to return to the small Hungarian town where he lived—and died—as a child. At this point it is evident that the movement by which a man generates a relation to himself is a movement of return. It is a return from exile, from east of Eden. In *The Town beyond the Wall* it is more than a return to the place of one's childhood: it is a return to oneself by offering oneself for the sake of another, just as the child is offered for the sake of the man, from the binding of Isaac at Moriah to the hanging of the little one at Buna. For when he returns to Hungary, Michael is picked up by the military police and must sustain their interrogations for three days to save Pedro. The man who had been victimized as a child returns to the place of his childhood and, like a child, becomes a victim for the sake of another. This is how the child shows the man the path that leads to himself: to become as a little child is to become a victim, to offer oneself for the sake of another. And the fact that the child *is* the way underscores the significance of the child as Messiah.

Thus Michael's example illustrates the messianic nature of the child within the man's relation to himself. Wiesel develops this messianic aspect of the child further in *The Testament,* a novel about a man whose quest for himself is inseparable from his quest for the Messiah. Like the story of Michael, Paltiel's story unfolds in a prison cell where he finds himself after having returned to the town where he lived as a child. It is from this cell that Paltiel writes,

> Such is the disquieting beauty of the messianic adventure: only man, for whose sake the Messiah is expected, is capable and worthy of making his advent possible. What man? Any man. Whosoever desires may seize the keys that open the gates of the celestial palace and thus bring power to the prisoner. The Messiah, you see, is a mystery between man and himself. [P. 72]

Why is it that the human being can make possible the advent of the Messiah? Because only the human being can exist as a child. This is a status unknown to God the Father; as soon as God becomes a child, he is no longer Father but Messiah, no longer God but God-man. As a child, the Messiah is the suffering God, and he becomes part of man's relation to himself by sharing in man's suffering. And since the human being alone can know the suffering of a child, only the human being can stand in relation to himself that turns on a relation to the Messiah.

In Michael we saw that the man's relation to himself lies in his relation to another; he becomes I by saying Thou. It will also be observed that Pedro is more than a friend to Michael—he is much like a father, a source of wisdom and guidance. Indeed, he is so much like the Father that at one point Michael asks him, "Tell me the truth, Pedro: are *you* God?" (p. 123). As with Michael, in Paltiel's case we see that the man's relation to the dead child within himself is inseparable from his relation to the father. Consider, for example, Paltiel's "lyrical, mystical vision" of his father at the head of a funeral procession:

> I ask him where he is going and he does not answer; I ask him whence he comes, he does not answer; . . . we walk in silence, but I hear someone talking to me; . . . I look before me and see

no one, and then I lower my eyes and see a little boy growing, growing; he motions to me, I recognize him; . . . he questions me without looking at me: "What have you made of me?" And behind him my father appears and he too motions to me and asks, "What have you made of me?" [Pp. 321–22]

In this passage from *The Testament* we find a developed idea that was only touched upon in *The Town Beyond the Wall*. Here we discover that if the child assumes the features of the Messiah, man's relation to the child is part of his relation to the father; and his relation to himself, his presence as a self, rests on his ability to respond to both. It will be recalled that in *One Generation After,* Wiesel has an exchange with another, who confesses that he was the one who killed the child; Paltiel shows us that as it goes with the child, so it goes with the father. If God is dead, it is because we have murdered him by murdering the child. Again, this murder is a suicide: to strike down God and child, to murder the Messiah, is to destroy all relation to oneself and thus lose oneself.

Paltiel's struggle to regenerate a relation to himself thus takes the form of regenerating a relation to the father by resurrecting the child. And he resurrects the child—and with the child, himself—by becoming a child. In *The Town Beyond the Wall,* Pedro asks Michael whether he wants to return to the place of his childhood to become "a child and die" (p. 103). In *The Testament* that is precisely what happens to Paltiel. "Returned to my cell," he says near the end, "I collapse. Finally alone, I become the child I never was, the orphan I shall cease to be. I weep for my father and I weep for my son, weep for my life and for my death" (p. 335). The cell that had been his tomb now becomes his womb. Emerging as the child he never was, Paltiel becomes Paltiel. This is the outcome of his testament, the fulfillment of his covenant, the end of his quest for the Messiah: to become himself by becoming a child.

Conclusion: Messianic Aspects of the Word

When Paltiel's father and the child in his vision ask him what he has made of them, he replies, "My collection of poems is my answer" (p. 322). Like Paltiel, Wiesel himself is a poet as well as a thinker. In *Legends of Our Time* he comments on his art, saying:

> For some, literature is a bridge linking childhood to death. While the one gives rise to anguish, the other invites nostalgia. The deeper the nostalgia and the more complete the fear, the purer, the richer the word and the secret.
> But for me writing is a *matzeva,* an invisible tombstone, erected to the memory of the dead unburied. Each word corresponds to a face, a prayer, the one needing the other so as not to sink into oblivion. [P. 25]

If Wiesel's literature does not link childhood to death, perhaps it may be said that it links death to the child. This certainly seems to be the case in his first work, *Night.* But because each word of his writing "corresponds to a face, a prayer," each word is a portal to redemption; this too Wiesel associates with the child. How does the child redeem the man? By returning him to himself as a child. And for Wiesel, as for Paltiel, this process is engendered by the Word.

Paltiel's friend and Messiah seeker David Aboulesia asserts that the story of the Messiah is the story of "a name in search of being" (p. 160). To be sure, this is what lies at the root of Wiesel's works; interwoven among the words and images, the tales and ideas, is a name in search of being. It is curled up in the questions with no answers, the questions that cry out from the ashes; it dwells in the silence and in the summons of the Word; it is the name of a child who calls to us and who listens for our call. Bearing this in mind may help us to listen more closely to Wiesel's remark on his works near the end of *Four Hasidic Masters:* "In retelling these tales, I realize once more that I owe them much. Consciously or not, I have incorporated a song, an echo, a word of theirs in my own legends and fables. I have remained, in a vanquished kingdom, a child who loves to listen." [15]

Thus examining the messianic aspects of the child in Wiesel's endeavors with the Word may reveal as much about the Word as it does about the child: if there is something of the Messiah about the child, the Word may also harbor its own messianic elements. For in the aftermath of the death of the child, we are left with a "blank, evil silence," to use Paltiel's words (p. 26), a silence in which, as he says, "one becomes isolated not only from mankind but from oneself" (p. 207). David Aboulesia tells him that a poet who does not look beyond the wall is like a bird without a song (p. 172). The wall is the wall of silence, and the Word is doorway to the beyond. As the thing that penetrates the wall, the Word returns man to a relation with his brother and therefore with himself; and, again, this return is his salvation. For as man is related to his brother and to himself—and to the child within each—so is he related to God and Messiah.

Paltiel's Quest for the Messiah in Wiesel's *The Testament*

HAVING EXAMINED THE FIGURE of the child as a messianic aspect of Wiesel's literature, let us now consider the concept of the Messiah as it unfolds in a particular work, *The Testament*, where we discover not only the messianic elements of literature but the messianic elements of literary language. Here too the child plays a prominent role in Wiesel's notion of the Messiah. Unlike Wiesel's earlier works, however, *The Testament* explores the significance of the Word and the individual's relation to the Father as integral facets of the search for the Messiah.

There are many authors in Western world literature who have undertaken the quest for the Messiah: Blake, Dostoevsky, Gide, and Kazantzakis are a few names that readily come to mind in this connection. Yet the Messiah himself remains as elusive and enigmatic as a question without an answer. Paltiel says in *The Testament,* "Among the ten things that preceded the Creation was the name of the Messiah—the name no one knows and no one will know before he appears." [1] Further, as the Messiah seeker David Aboulesia explains to the young Paltiel: "His name, which preceded Creation, also preceded him. The story of the Messiah is the story of a quest, of a name in search of being" (p. 160). *The Testament* provides a clue to why the Messiah remains—and must remain—a figure without a name and a name in search of being, why the story

of the Messiah is a story of a quest. Through the tale of Paltiel
Kossover, Wiesel shows that the Messiah is not an individual
but an event in precisely the sense that the Word is an event.
The Messiah is not a person or an entity that can be tagged
with a name and thereby lost to the name; no, he is rather the
struggle for the name and the name's struggle for being: the
Messiah is the quest for the Messiah.

Conceived as a quest, the Messiah is like a bridge spanning
the chasm that cuts through the self who is in need of redemption. The Messiah, says Paltiel, "is a mystery between man
and himself" (p. 72), and the mystery is what sets man in
motion. Understanding this movement through the space between man and himself, this tension between the poles, is essential to understanding the Messiah in terms of a quest; indeed,
this movement, this tension, this attempt to intone the Word is
the quest itself. An examination of Paltiel's quest, therefore,
must focus on those aspects of his story that position him
within a structure of movement. Wiesel's novel deals with
three relations, which are interwoven, and which place Paltiel
in a situation of existing in-between: the relation to the Father
on one side, to the Child on the other, and to the Word pulsat-
ing between the two. These are the ingredients of Paltiel's
quest for the Messiah in Wiesel's *The Testament*.

Paltiel's Relation to the Father

In a letter to his son, Grisha, Paltiel writes: "I do not know
what life is, and I shall die without knowing. My father, whose
name you bear, knew. But he is dead" (p. 20). If the Messiah
is a mystery between man and himself, the father is the one
who holds the key to the mystery. He is the seed of Abraham
who bears the seed of Abraham: he is the keeper of the Covenant. To be sure, one meaning of the word *testament* is "a
covenant with God." But the father is dead—or exiled: Paltiel's father's name is Gershon, from Gershom, meaning "the
exiled." Paltiel, then, is a child born in the wilderness; like
his father, he is an exile living on the edges of the Promised

Land. Although his father knew what life is, Paltiel must set out on the quest for life. Because the father knows what life is, it is he who guides Paltiel's quest. Yes, Paltiel associates with Communist Jews; he writes for them and even carries out missions for them. Yet, like a man clinging to a lifeline as he descends into the deep, he clings to the phylacteries that bind him to the Father. And as he penetrates the depths, he looks up now and then for the light that shines from the eye of the father.

In his description of his mission to Palestine, for example, Paltiel comments, "From the beginning to end, my father's eyes never left me" (p. 185). The eye of the father not only guides—it judges. The figure of the father is the figure of the Law; his is the power and authority to bestow the blessing and to mete out the judgment. Paltiel's consciousness of being looked upon, moreover, brings him before himself in judgment of himself; he scrutinizes himself through the eyes of the father and, inevitably, does not like what he sees. He does not know what the father knows, and this is why he undertakes his search, which is haunted by his father's secret. The dilemma that the judgment of the eyes brings upon him, the dilemma that divides him, is this: because he does not know what life is, he is guilty—not only of not knowing but of trying to find out. Paltiel has chosen a path not in keeping with that of his fathers; he is gathering his knowledge from a forbidden tree.

But Paltiel's rebellion runs deeper than simply following a different way. Having taken up the way of communism, he has embraced a messianism without God, and this constitutes a revolt against the father. Like Absalom rising up against David in the name of a justice that cannot be, Paltiel leaves behind his father and the God of his fathers for the sake of an -ism that holds the promise of justice, the promise of "from each according to his ability, to each according to his need." Thus he chooses to place himself under the eye of a different father figure, even though he still longs for the eye of the Father to show him the way. While in the Russian army during the Second World War, for example, Paltiel stands at attention as a general looks him over. When the general scans him from boot to cap, Paltiel's thoughts return to his birthplace, to the small Russian town of Barassy, where once again he comes before his father; but his father has trouble recognizing the son who now wears the insignia of the Red Army in the place of the phylacteries (p. 267).

The point to be noted in this connection, however, is that Paltiel's thoughts do return to his father and to the home of his early childhood. Although he has donned the costume of communism, his heart remains planted in the soil from which something of the seed of Abraham has sprung. This link with the father is the one tie that binds Paltiel to life at a time when he is engulfed by death, when death is extinguishing every flame except the one by which it is illuminated. Unable to bring himself to destroy life, Paltiel becomes a medic, haunting the graveyard that the world has become. "I lived in a kind of trance," he says. "I no longer sought the living; only the dead interested me. I was their companion, their savior" (p. 285). And how is Paltiel resurrected from this world of the dead? Listen: "I felt lost. Abandoned. Was there anyone left to turn to? I was climbing a mountain of ashes. On the other side an old man was waiting. And he was saying, 'Come, my son. Come'" (p. 285) That his father becomes his deliverance is clearer still when Paltiel alludes to the interrogation that followed his arrest, saying, "Whenever I weakened and felt I was about to yield, my father appeared in a dream and saved me" (p. 334). If we recall that the name *Paltiel*—the name bestowed upon him by the Father—means "God is my deliverance," then we may see that Paltiel's relation to the father is inseparable from his relation to the God of his fathers. Like the God of Abraham, Isaac, and Jacob, the father knows the way, calls to judgment, and delivers from death.

Further, because the son is of the father, Paltiel's relation to the father is a definitive element of his relation to himself. The estrangement from his father that Paltiel experiences on his quest, then, is also an estrangement from himself. This link between the relation to the father and the relation to the self may be found, for instance, in these two stanzas from one of Paltiel's poems:

In my dream
my father
asked me
if he is still
my father.
[P. 294]

And:

And so I see my father
in my dream
and fail to see
myself.
[Pp. 294–95]

Because the father knows what life is, Paltiel looks to him to determine what his own life is; any sense of self that Paltiel may have arises from the recognition gained from the father—or from the absence of it. When, for example, his Russian unit enters Liyanov, the small Romanian town where Paltiel had left his parents behind years earlier, he finds his father's house, but his family is gone, dead: "A mad idea shoots through me: the house is my house, but I . . . I am not I" (p. 288).

The I who is not I is the I who has lost his relation to the father. It is the dead self—dead because the father is dead—whom Paltiel seeks to resurrect. One instance of the connection between the absence of the relation to the father and the death of the self may be found in Paltiel's "lyrical, mystical vision," in which he sees his father leading a funeral procession. "I ask him where he is going," Paltiel explains, "and he does not answer" (p. 321). His father does not answer him because it is his, Paltiel's, funeral. The lost self, the dead self, is the self who seeks a word of redemption from the father; yet as long as the self is lost, it meets only with silence. When Paltiel lies wounded in a military hospital, for instance, he imagines himself calling upon and even accusing God, but his "words met a stony silence. God chose not to respond." When a friend who heard his address to God asks what he wants,

Paltiel answers, "Redemption," adding, "In this place I have
the right to demand and receive everything; and what I demand
is redemption." To which his companion replies: "So do I.
And so does He" (p. 316). The problem confronting Paltiel,
then, is how to find the redemption which both he and the
father desire and which can be had only through a relation to
the father. Both long for the relation, but neither can generate
it alone. The relation to the father must therefore rest on another relation.

Paltiel's Relation to the Child

Paltiel seeks life by seeking recognition and redemption from
the father, but he acknowledges the child as the one who binds
him to life. Recall these words cited in the last chapter: "Let
us not speak of Raissa, Citizen Magistrate. She is not the one
who binds me to life; it is my son Grisha. Will I see him again
one day? Will I ever speak to him of my father, whose name
he bears?" (p. 147). If the father is someone to answer to, the
child is someone to live for. Paltiel's son binds him to life
because his son represents the life he is capable of bringing
into the world, the life he imparts to life; his son represents his
ability to carry on the Creation, to continue and thus be a part
of the seed of Abraham. And this draws him nearer to the God
of Abraham, the God for whom all things are possible. The
child binds Paltiel to life by instilling his life with possibility
and value. As with God, with the child everything is possible;
without the child, nothing has value (cf. p. 70).

It should be noted at this point that Paltiel's relation to the
child is not confined to his relation to his son. As a medic
during the Second World War, for example, he sets out to
glean the living from the dead like a man saving children from
the gullet of some dreaded monster. Indeed, in the midst of
battle he speaks of and addresses the wounded as if they were
children: "He was beautiful, and light as a child. I spoke to
him as I always did, repeating what I always said to my dead:
Don't worry, my little one, we are almost there" (p. 307). And

if we follow this scene further, we discover something more
about Paltiel's relation to the child:

> My guardian angel on my shoulders, I moved forward, tripping.
> Then I was lifted off the ground. Violent red pain. I opened my
> eyes: the impact had thrown me into a trench. Torn to bits, he was
> nothing but a decapitated, legless corpse. He had saved my life: I
> was only wounded. [Pp. 307–308]

Here, as in the previous chapter, we catch a glimpse of a messianic aspect of the Child. Like a man resurrected from the
grave, Paltiel rises from the trench, ransomed by the life of
the "little one" who was "light as a child." He is related to
the child, then, as a man is related to his savior, and he is
saved precisely because he set out to save the child. His guardian angel? Not a figure of sword and flame but a child, small,
frail, and helpless.

Thus, like the father who appeared in a dream and saved
him, the child too saves Paltiel. At this juncture it becomes
more clear that the relation to the father is definitively concerned with the relation to the child. And we see it more
clearly still when we find Paltiel donning the phylacteries for
his child as he had done for his father: "The next day I put on
the phylacteries again. This time I waited until Grisha woke
up. He pulled at the straps, and that filled me with great joy"
(p. 332). The image of the little hands clinging to the straps
suggests a child holding on to keep from falling—or is it to
keep his father from falling? The lifeline is there, but who is
saving whom? The little one is saving his father. For it is the
child who imparts great joy to the father, and there is nothing
more redeeming than this joy, a joy steeped in love.

It was noted above that Paltiel's name means "God is my
deliverance." Here one discovers that the child is equally the
man's deliverance; God delivers man by becoming a child. For
the first time since he himself was a child, Paltiel, as he leans
over his baby, is joyful, at one with himself; it is as if his child
had reached out and healed a deep wound that had cut through
his soul. The divided self who had sought redemption from the
father now discovers it in the child. Moreover, the child shows

Paltiel the way to salvation by showing him the way to the
child within. To be sure, Paltiel has been seeking himself as a
child all along. We find an indication of this, for instance,
when he mentions his parents' desire for him to return to Liyanov, saying: "The Jew in me wanted to follow their call, to
kiss their hands, to rediscover his childhood. But the communist prevailed" (p. 243). That his relation to the child he was
characterizes his relation to the child is further demonstrated
by the vision of his father in the funeral procession:

> I wait for the procession to pass and I follow it at a distance—we
> walk, we walk in silence, but I hear someone talking to me and I
> know I am forbidden to know who it is; I look before me and see
> no one, then I lower my eyes and see a little boy growing, grow-
> ing; he motions to me, I recognize him; he questions me without
> saying a word—and I understand that it was his silence that had
> spoken to me earlier—he questions me without looking at me:
> "What have you made of me?" [Pp. 321–22]

The one who calls him to reckoning—not to judgment but to
reckoning—is not a terrible figure seated on a heavenly throne
but the child he was, the child who abides within, silently,
imploringly.

The voice—or the silence—of the child within is what beckons Paltiel to return, to become the child he has lost. This
movement of return, in fact, marks the outcome of his quest
as he nears death: "Returned to my cell, I collapse. Finally
alone, I become the child I never was, the orphan I shall cease
to be. I weep for my father and I weep for my son, I weep for
my life and for my death" (p. 335). It will be noted that Paltiel
is returned to his cell like a man laid into a tomb; but, as is
often the case, there is a relation between tomb and womb, for
the cell is also the place where the child he never was is born,
the place where Paltiel is reborn. The claim that Paltiel does
indeed become a child at the end of his quest is further sup-
ported by the secretary Zupanev's repeated reference to him as
"your big child of a father" in his final remarks to Grisha
(pp. 337, 346).

Zupanev is a witness entrusted with Paltiel's testament, a messenger on a mission from Paltiel to Grisha. "He made me care,"

says Zupanev of Paltiel. "He even made me laugh, me, who never laughed in all my life" (p. 204). And recall Zupanev's statement near the end of the novel: "And suddenly it happens: I am laughing, I am laughing at last. . . . It's idiotic, even unjust, but it is the dead, the dead poets who will force men like me and all others to laugh" (p. 346). This is exactly how Paltiel makes him into a witness: by making him laugh. As the one who recorded Paltiel's words, Zupanev is the keeper of the voice that comes from Paltiel and from beyond him. The figure of Zupanev as the bearer of the Word that links father and child provides us with a hint of the function of the Word as that which joins the father and the child in the messianic mission.

Paltiel's Relation to the Word

If deliverance means freedom, then like the father and like the child, the Word is also Paltiel's deliverance. In his letter to Grisha, for example, Paltiel indicates that the Word brings him freedom even within the confines of his prison cell: "I can write as much as I like. And what I like. I'm a free man" (p. 19). Paltiel's writing frees him because it provides him with a link to his father and to his son; it instills him with a voice, with a presence, so that he is not left to founder in the silent enclosures of self and solitude. As he allows the Word to speak through him, he is able to hear his father say to him, "Remember this, Paltiel: with God everything is possible; without Him nothing has value" (p. 70). It may also be recalled that the title of Paltiel's one volume of poetry is *I Saw My Father in a Dream,* alluding to a vision made real by the Word which is its vessel. Examining the vision of his father in his dream more closely, one finds that Paltiel's link to his father is the same as his link to his son: "I see you, my son, as I see my father. I see you both as in a dream, and the dream is real" (p. 19). Again, Paltiel is a free man because the Word creates for him this common bond with father and child.

The Word not only frees Paltiel *for* a relation to the father and to the child—it frees him *from* death. He notes, for in-

stance, that "King David used to love to sing, and as long as
he sang, the Angel of Death could not approach him; composing his Psalms, he was immortal" (p. 30). In this regard it
should be noted that the real death is the living death, the death
of emptiness and absence of self; as Wiesel has remarked in
The Oath, "There are men who are dead and do not know it." [2]
Song is existence, song is life, song is the opposite of death;
and Paltiel Kossover is a singer. Consider, for example, the
following exchange between Grisha and his mother, Raissa:

> "Remember—your father is a poet."
> "What does that mean?"
> "It means poets live in the present."
> "What does that mean?"
> "It means that . . . For him, life was a song. He thought every-
> thing could be accomplished through words. . . .
> "Dead? My father? How is that possible, if he is a poet? You
> told me poets live forever."
> "They do."
> "Well then . . ."
> "They are dead, but they live on."
> "No, Mommy. My father is not dead. My father is a book, and
> books do not die." [P. 39]

Once again we find that, like the father, like the child, the
Word binds Paltiel to life. It constitutes him not only as book,
not only as song, but as testament, as a promise kept and
passed on. It instills him with the resonance of substance, with
the peal of silence.

Paltiel's relation to the Word, then, is a relation to silence. [3]
It is a relation that cuts through the silence of the father and of
the Child. As a child, for example, Paltiel had a teacher and
father figure named Rebbe Mendel-the-Taciturn, with whose
help he "pursued silence in words and words in silence" (*Testament,* p. 71). Paltiel's own child, Grisha, a poet "not like his
father" but "in place of his father" (p. 17), is a mute who also
pursues silence in words and words in silence. Indeed, for
Grisha, silence is a living sanctuary, where the soul of his
father and his own soul abide, a sanctuary over which he keeps
a most stern vigil: in order to protect it at a moment when it

was threatened, he bit off his tongue (pp. 304–305). In Grisha's case, the silence of the mute is not a mute silence. Here the Word is alive in the silence of the child, and Paltiel lives in this silence. It is like the silence in the town of Worke, which Wiesel has described as "an appeal, an outcry to God on behalf of his desperate people and also on his behalf, an offering to night, to heaven, an offering made by wise old men and quiet children to mark the end of language—the outer limits of creation—a burning secret buried in silence."[4] Such is the silence Paltiel speaks of when he says to the Citizen Magistrate: "The words you strangle, the words you murder, produce a kind of primary, impenetrable silence. And you will never succeed in killing a silence such as this" (p. 30). Paltiel's relation to the Word thus instills silence with a redemptive power, with the power of a voice; his relation to the Word makes silence the mitigator of his solitude and part of the link underlying his relation to the father and to the child.

But if silence can mitigate, it can also isolate. Let us listen to Paltiel:

> As a child in Barassy, as an adolescent in Liyanov, I yearned for silence. . . . I begged God to find me a mute master who would impart his truth—and his words—to me worldlessly. I spent hours with a disciple of the Hasidic school of Worke, whose rebbe had turned silence into a method. . . . Later, with Rebbe Mendel-the-Taciturn, we tried to transcend language. At midnight, our eyes closed, our faces turned toward Jerusalem and its fiery sanctuary, we listened to the song of its silence—a celestial and yet terrible silence in which both voices and moments attain immortality.
>
> No master had ever warned me that silence could be nefarious, evil. . . . No master had ever told me that silence could become a prison.
>
> You have taught me more than my masters, Citizen Magistrate. In this "isolator"—the word is well chosen: in it one becomes isolated not only from mankind but from oneself—I have attained a level of knowledge I had despaired of reaching. [P. 207]

Here one must note the difference between the silence that speaks to the child and the silence that threatens the man in search of the child. As a child—before he became a poet in pursuit of words—Paltiel's relation to the Word made silence sing. But when his relation to the Word becomes a quest for the Word, silence points up the inner division behind his quest. "It invades, dominates, and reduces man to slavery," says Paltiel. "And once a slave of silence, you are no longer a man" (p. 209). Yes, he acquires a knowledge he had despaired of attaining, but it is the knowledge acquired in the Fall, the knowledge that marks the death of the child. Thus the poet endeavors to resurrect the child by pursuing the Word that may enable him to hear silence sing the song of his resurrection, the song that will return him to human being.

Paltiel's relation to the Word is therefore a definitive aspect of his relation to the child, which, as we have seen, is the foundation of his relation to the father. Recalling the end of Paltiel's vision of the funeral procession, we see more clearly that all three relations are of a piece:

> I lower my eyes and see a little boy growing, growing; he motions to me, I recognize him; he questions me without saying a word— and I understand that it was his silence that had spoken to me earlier—he questions me without looking at me: "What have you made of me?" And behind him my father appears and he too motions to me and asks, "What have you made of me?" And my collection of poems is my answer. [Pp. 321–22]

Paltiel's relation to the father and to the child is created by his relation to the Word, and his relation to the Word is what generates his relation to himself: the Word is what enables him to say, "Here I am." To be sure, for Paltiel, as for anyone on a quest, the question of who he is cannot be distinguished from the question of where he is. Zupanev tells Grisha, for example, that when Paltiel came before the magistrate, the first thing he wanted to know was where he had been brought and not why he had been brought there: "Later he explained. 'Some people define themselves in relation to what they do—not me. I define myself in relation to the place where I happen to be'" (p. 205).

Paltiel's relation to the Word thus leads him to a concept of self defined by relation to something or someone outside of himself. Implying both the separation and the union of two, the Word situates the I before the Thou, and the self emerges in the tension, in the polarity, between the two. As Buber has pointed out: "There is in reality no I except the I of a tension: in which it brings itself together. No pole, no force, no thing—only polarity, only stream, only unification can become I." [5] Further, the geographical peregrinations of Paltiel's quest parallel the movement and the flow created by the Word; the movements of the quest are inseparable from the movements of the Word. Any I that Paltiel may become is the I of a movement, and the Word engenders the relation that gives the movement direction. Paltiel situates two poles—the father and the child—and dwells in the tension between them, dwells in the Word, which is the house of his being.

The Quest for the Messiah

With these three dimensions of Paltiel's quest for the Messiah before us—the relation to the father, to the child, and to the Word—two questions must be asked. First, exactly what event occurs in his quest for the Messiah? And what can be said about the identity of the Messiah?

The story of Paltiel's quest for the Messiah is the story of a single event: the transfiguration of the father into the child through the Word. This may be seen first of all in the fact that Paltiel's father and child both bear the same name: Gershon. Remember, too, Paltiel's words as he bends over to kiss his infant child: "May God be with you, Son; may God remain with you, Father" (p. 330). And: "I hid in the eyes of my son as I had once taken refuge in those of my father" (p. 332). Moreover, the emergence of this identity between father and child may be found in other places in the novel, particularly in the final pages, where the quest nears its culmination. It will be observed, for example, that in Paltiel's "lyrical, mystical vision" both father and child put the same question to him and that he has a single answer for the two of them, as though he were responding not only to one question but to one voice.

Further, at the moment when Paltiel is about to be taken to prison and to death, we read:

> I thought of my father and of my son *at the same time*. The same thought enveloped them both, the same desire to protect them. I was overwhelmed by remorse: I had lived without being able to help them. And I was afraid: judged by either one of them, what could I say in my defense? [P. 333]

Finally, it should be pointed out that the transfiguration of the father into the child happens to Paltiel himself immediately before his death and the end of his quest: "Returned to my cell, I collapse. Finally alone, I become the child I never was, the orphan I shall cease to be" (p. 335).

What, then, can be said about the identity of the Messiah, the object of Paltiel's quest? We can begin to answer this question by thinking of the Messiah as the child Paltiel never was. Or better: the Messiah is the event marked by the transfiguration of the father into the child through the Word. The quest for the Messiah is a fallen man's quest for the child. Wiesel, in fact, explicitly evokes this identity of child and Messiah elsewhere. In *The Oath,* for instance, we hear Moshe declare: "The Messiah. . . . We seek him, we pursue him. We think he is in heaven; we don't know that he likes to come down as a child. And yet, every man's childhood is messianic in essence" (p. 132).

In *The Testament* there is also an indication of this identity, but it is much more subtle. Just as the Messiah dons the disguise of a child, Wiesel disguises the identity of the child and the Messiah with a name. This occurs when Paltiel alludes to the sounds reverberating through the streets of Jerusalem, saying: "A mother's strident cry: 'Ahmad, are you coming?' And a child answers, 'Coming, coming'" (p. 190). As always, Wiesel's use of a name, no matter how casual it may seem, is calculated and laden with meaning: the name Ahmad is a variant of Ahmed, which signifies the Paraclete.[6] Who, then, answers, "Coming, coming," to the strident cry? It is the Comforter, he who intercedes, the One who is already among us, in quest of us when we are not in quest of him.

Given the significance of Jerusalem in Wiesel's writings, the fact that Paltiel hears this voice of a child in Jerusalem is also to be noted. Recall, for example, these lines from *A Beggar in Jerusalem:* "Jerusalem: the face visible yet hidden, the sap and the blood of all that makes us live or renounce life. The spark in the darkness, the murmur rustling through shouts of happiness and joy. A name, a secret." [7] And, as David Aboulesia asserts to the young Paltiel, the story of the Messiah is the story of "a name in search of being" (p. 160). The quest? A name struggling to be pronounced so that a child may answer, "Coming, coming."

A Final Word

Hence in Wiesel's *The Testament* the event that characterizes Paltiel's quest and the event by which the Messiah is constituted are one and the same. Perhaps now the claim made at the outset may be understood more clearly. Says the Messiah seeker Aboulesia, "The great thing is not to be the Messiah but to seek him" (p. 163): the Messiah is the quest for the Messiah.

But we are not quite finished. That Paltiel undertook his messianic quest by pursuing communism is also significant, especially in the light of Azriel's statement in *The Oath:* "You want to know what communism is? It is messianism without God, just as Christianity is messianism without man" (p. 73). We may now elaborate on this by saying that communism is messianism without the father, while Christianity has become messianism without the child. And in each case the absence of father and child points up the absence of the Word. The sign of the absence of the Word in Christianity and in communism is this: both claim to have found the answer, the truth, the last word, and neither is engaged in a quest, though each is bent on the conversion of the world. They seek not the response of a Thou but the acquiescence of the crowd. They have come to a stop, paralyzed by the truths that have degenerated into complacent judgments.

And what about the Jew? This is what Wiesel says in *One Generation After:* "The Jew is in perpetual motion. He is characterized as much by his quest as by his faith, his silence as much as his outcry. He defines himself more by what troubles him than by what reassures him. . . . To me, the Jew and his questioning are one."[8] And in *The Town beyond the Wall* he applies this notion not only to the Jew but to man: "The essence of man is to be a question, and the essence of the question is to be without answer."[9] And in *The Testament* Paltiel says: "All that remains is faith. God. As a source of questioning I would gladly accept Him; but what He requires is affirmation, and there I must draw the line. And yet. . . ." (p. 20). Wherever quest and questioning are alive, so is the Word, and this is what lies behind Paltiel's "And yet"; indeed, we have seen that Paltiel lives in the Word, in his poetry, because he is a man characterized as much by his quest as by his faith. We have also seen that his quest is shaped by his relation to the father and to the child; and what does that relation consist of? Love. Love, then, is the essence of the quest; says Wiesel in *The Accident,* "Love is a question mark, not an exclamation point."[10] It is in the question, in the quest, that love and the Word find their single presence. For where the Word is absent, love is absent. In communism and Christianity alike, love has been eclipsed by doctrine and the Word by words, words, words: both insist that all who do not subscribe to the letter of their dogma are lost.

It would be appropriate to close, then, with these lines from Feuerbach:

> God is love, but because of his love, of the *predicate,* is it that he renounced his Godhead; thus love is a higher power and truth than deity. Love conquers God. . . . Who then is our Saviour and Redeemer? God or Love? Love; for God as God has not saved us, but Love, which transcends the difference between the divine and human personality. As God has renounced himself out of love, so we, out of love, should renounced God; for if we do not sacrifice God to love, we sacrifice love to God, and, in spite of the predicate of love, we have the God—the evil being—of religious fanaticism.[11]

It was neither Judaism nor communism nor any other -ism that engendered Paltiel's relation to the father, to the child, and to the Word. No, it was his love for each that provided the impetus for his quest. His Savior? His Messiah? Love. Perhaps that was the revelation he had in mind when he ended his testament with the mysterious words, "I shall tell Grisha what I have never yet revealed to anyone; I shall tell him that . . . " (p. 336).

CHAPTER NINE

Conclusion

IN THIS BOOK we have scratched a few surfaces of the dialogical Word that links religion, language, and literature. It is now time to consider how we might respond to the three questions raised in the introductory chapter, questions that correspond to the three parts of this book. The questions are: What does regarding the word as spirit imply about how we regard literature? What is literature's capacity for dealing with the religious dimension of life? And what impact may literature have on a human being's relation to God and to other human beings? Before proceeding, it must be kept in mind that no response to these questions will settle them. The purpose of concluding with a response to the questions raised is not to eliminate them but to sustain them. For in sustaining the question, we maintain our responsive, dialogical presence in relation to the ties that bind religion, language, and literature; we maintain the movement that characterizes presence.

What Does Regarding the Word as Spirit Imply About How We Regard Literature?

Throughout this book, from Saint John to Elie Wiesel, the dialogical Word has been viewed as spirit. Approached in this way, the dialogical Word is what Buber calls the basic word, *I-Thou,* the Word that underlies relation, life's attachment to life, summons and response. It is a portal to all giving and

152

receiving, to love of that which is all love, to the affirmation of what there is to live and die for. The dialogical Word makes up the language that joins rather than isolates. It is the Word that Lacan takes to be the language of the self and the Word that failed Golyadkin in Dostoevsky's *Dvoinik*. It is the discourse that, on Bakhtin's view, constitutes our endless effort to speak the truth. It is the Word by which Wiesel struggles to sustain a faith in God, to say no in such a way that it means yes, and to remain a relentless witness to what must never be forgotten.

Literature regarded as dialogical Word is literature regarded as Johannine logos, as a voice that calls forth the life of those who have ears to hear. This means that whatever spiritual life we have is grounded in literature's dialogical Word. It means that each time we come before a literary text, no matter how many times we have stood before it, we are summoned anew to answer for our spiritual presence in life; it means that our relation to literature and to the life it invokes is never settled. If Word is spirit, then literature, whose substance is the Word, must be regarded as spirit, as that which summons life's attachment to life and love of that which is all love. Such a view of literature has serious implications for our relation to it. If, for example, that relation is strictly aesthetic, structural, or ideological, then we betray the Word and the life into which it breathes its life. If our relation to literature does not enhance our affirmation and embrace of the Thou before us, if it does not lead us to reckoning and accountability, if it does not add to our love for a child—then we have lost the literature and, with it, ourselves.

All of the figures we have examined, each in his own way, view literature in terms of responsibility. All of them have heard a summons from the other side or from the inside and struggle to open our ears to that summons. They represent examples of those who conceive of literature as a message in a bottle, which we, as castaways, receive from the other shore; indeed, they themselves are messengers and would make us into messengers. If we regard the Word as spirit, then we approach literature not as critics but as witnesses who are then transformed into messengers. If in part one we began with literary logos and literary criticism, we ended with Word as spirit and critic as witness. No longer do we come before a text, before the letter, which is the dead flesh of meaning. No, we come before the countenance, before the living spirit, which imparts meaning to life by making us answerable for the meaning we impart to life. The question is not what we can get out of the text but what the text can get out of us.

Thus part one, along with the question that corresponds to it, leaves us without the firm ground of objective method and turns us over to the shifting ground of subjective response. Literature becomes a Thou who addresses us from the page and from beyond the page, a life that poses for us the task of embracing life. This is a religious view of literature rooted in a religious concept of language, a view that brings us from part one to part two and the next question.

What Is Literature's Capacity for Dealing with the Religious Dimension of Life?

The religious dimension of life, again, is where life generates its attachment to life; without a religious dimension, there is no human life. The thing that characterizes the attachment is the question about what is most needful, a question that creates its strongest bond when it is unsettled. To ask about the religious dimension of life is to ask about the open-ended questions we put to ourselves; it is to ask about truth or meaning which is *not yet*. We may recall that Bakhtin's concern with the novel arises from such questions. Buber and Wiesel also embrace a religious concept of language and literature, which rests on a question: Where are you? The matter of literature's ability to deal with the religious dimension of life, then, is a matter involving literature's ability to deal with questions about life's attachment to life.

At this point I will state explicitly what I suggested in the introductory chapter and implied throughout the book: literature and literature alone can address the religious dimension of life. In a sense—but only in a sense—literature *is* the religious dimension of life. From the songs of the myth makers to Wiesel's literary response to the Holocaust, the human endeavor to live in a religious mode has been an endeavor to live in a literary mode. The speculative thought that distinguishes philosophy and theology, the scientific method that characterizes psychology and sociology, these cannot begin to grasp the outcry that is the mark of religious life. Indeed, outcry cannot be grasped at all; at best, it can only be responded to. It is no coincidence that many so-called philosophers who operate in the fear and trembling of religious concern—Kierkegaard, Nietzsche, Buber, and Camus, for example—either regard themselves as poets or undertake some form of literary activity to address the questions they raise.

Perhaps the most important thing that testifies to literature's capacity for dealing with the religious dimension of life is its effort and its ability to name the Nameless and to reveal the Unmanifest. In this connection we may note Bakhtin's insistence that the ultimate Word is never uttered and Wiesel's emphasis on the significance of silence to language. To be sure, the religious concept of language and literature addressed in part two leads us to a religious concept of silence, transforming silence from an empty blank into a vibrant presence. In a literary text what is left unsaid, what the voice leaves to silence, is always as essential to the message as the words themselves. The words form a space, a chamber, within which the silence can resonate, and in that silence we encounter the religious dimension of life. Think of the silence of Abraham on the way to Moriah and the silence of Jesus before Pilate. Think of the silence of Grisha in Wiesel's *The Testament*.

The movement from the literary logos to a religious concept of language and literature, then, is a movement from Word as spirit to silence as presence. Literature's ability to deal with the religious dimension of life is an ability to embody both word and silence. It is a capacity for dealing with questions that surround birth, death, and resurrection—those moments in our lives when silence is most called for and most calls out to us. Resurrection, moreover, entails some notion of salvation and redemption, salvation from the letter, which kills, and redemption to the spirit, which gives life. This is the literary project; this is literature's mission. And because it is a mission of redemption and return to life, it is messianic in essence. As such, literature has profound implications for the relation between man and God and between man and man. Thus we arrive at the third question under consideration.

What Impact May Literature Have on the Human Being's Relation to God and to Other Human Beings?

This question provides a bridge that links part two with part three. The religious dimension of life is the dimension of relation between the human I and the eternal Thou, a relation that finds its expression between one human being and another. A religious concept of language and literature points up the unity of the human and divine relations. There is but one relation. Love of God and love of neighbor are of a piece; he who loves, loves God. And because the human joins with the divine through the literary, dialogical Word, literature and language take on messianic features. In chapter 2, on the Johannine logos, the messianic element of the Word is quite pronounced. Yet the concern with the Messiah in that chapter is not so far removed from the perspective on the Messiah in chapter 8 as it may seem. In chapter 8 the Messiah is viewed as the quest for the Messiah, the truth as the search for the truth, and love as the love of that which is all love. Love, in fact, is the bond that connects the first and last chapters in this book. And love is the name of literature's impact on the human being's relation to God and to other human beings.

Literature is love. It is the stuff of which love's body is made. We would be hard pressed to find a work of literature that does not entail some form of love between man and woman, man and God, or man and fellow man. That the figure of the child is so prominent in part three should also be remembered in this connection. For literature's impact on the life of relation is much like the impact of the child. The coming of the child is the highest expression of the love between man and woman. That God becomes a child is the highest expression of the love between God and humanity. And the love of one human being for a fellow human being is at its highest when it is a childlike love, never judging, totally trusting, and all forgiving. This is the messianic love, and it comprises the messianic elements of language and literature.

To say that literature's impact on relation lies in the love it brings to relation is to say that literature instills relation with spirit. Literature breathes spiritual life into what would otherwise be the dust of death. In so doing, literature and the literary Word redeem and resurrect life, so that literature has a messianic impact on the relation between one human being and another, between the human being and God. In a sense, the Messiah is a literary figure couched in the literary Word, who transforms words to make literature's impact on life a salvific one. Like the face of a newborn child, each utterance of the literary Word rises up from the void of silence to summon us from the void of absence. We receive the summons and our salvation from absence only through a response that cannot be prepared or calculated beforehand. No -ism or method will do. And every attempt to devise a new artifice for dealing with literature only adds more stone and mortar to the wall that cuts us off from literature's offering to the life of relation.

There is a Hasidic saying that God enters where he is allowed to enter. So it is with literature: it has an impact on the relation between human being and God, between human being and human being, where it is allowed to have an impact. But the movements in literary criticism and literary theory that currently dominate the world's intellectual community are largely efforts to remain deaf to literature's summons, to construct a fortress that the literary Word cannot penetrate. True, the focus on language is in vogue, and literary theory is all the rage. But, as Johathan Culler pointed out in a lecture at the University of Oklahoma on November 11, 1984, to seriously bring up religion in connection with literature is often considered unsophisticated and sophomoric. In that lecture Culler did indeed bring up religion—as the thing that must be extricated from literary study, except as a cultural curiosity. Yet to purge literature of religion is to purge language of the Word, to purge life of its attachment to life, leaving nothing but a wasteland populated by hollow men.

Most literary critics and theorists today bespeak the exile of the Word. Eliminating or ignoring religion in their concern with language and literature, they lose the dialogical Word and, with it, the very thing their subject has to offer to life. For all their labor, they are left only with the folded arms of complacency instead of the open arms of embrace. The intellectual experience has taken over the life-and-death enterprise. God is hiding, as a Hasidic master once lamented, and no one is looking for him. And so it will remain as long as literary study is merely a matter of prestige, publication, and promotion. Making religion part of the link between language and literature, however, means more than adding it as an object of investigation. Religion must become not something we know but something we are, and our critical response must be more in the nature of prayer than of commentary or explanation. Religion, language, literature—when they are bound by the dialogical Word—find their way into every facet of the life we offer and receive. They shape the way we greet the day and bury the dead; they are included in every extension of the hand, in every laugh, in every tear.

So where does all this leave us? Coming to the end of this book, we come to an edge. It is the edge between the words on the page and the life that begins where those words leave off; it is the edge between conceptualizing the integration of religion, language, and literature and actualizing it. Just as the truth can never be written, no bonding through the dialogical Word can ever be achieved in a book. Does that mean this project has failed? I think not. For whatever is to become real must first be imagined; deeds are things grown from ideas; and to discover is to impart. The task that remains is the most difficult: to bear living witness to the interrelation of religion, language, and literature—to burn with the affirming flame.

Notes

Chapter 1

1. Ludwig Feuerbach, *The Essence of Christianity,* trans. George Eliot (New York: Harper & Row, 1957), p. 332.

2. Miguel de Unamuno, *Tragic Sense of Life,* trans. J. E. Crawford Flitch (New York: Dover Publications, 1954), p. 218.

3. Henri Bergson, *The Two Sources of Morality and Religion,* trans. R. Ashley Audra and Cloudsley Brereton (Garden City, N.Y.: Doubleday, 1954), pp. 210, 212. Subsequent quotations are from this book.

4. Joseph Campbell, *The Masks of God: Primitive Mythology* (New York: Viking Press, 1959), p. 472.

5. Susan A. Handelman, *The Slayers of Moses* (Albany: State University of New York Press, 1982), p. 63. Subsequent quotations are from this book.

6. Herbert Schneidau, *Sacred Discontent* (Berkeley: University of California Press, 1976), p. 31. Subsequent quotations are from this book.

7. Jacques Derrida, *De la grammatologie* (Paris: Les Éditions de Minuit, 1967), p. 41. Author's translation. Unless otherwise noted, all other translations are the author's. Subsequent quotations are from this book.

8. Martin Heidegger, *Poetry, Language, Thought,* trans. Albert Hofstadter (New York: Harper & Row, 1971), p. 94. Subsequent quotations are from this book.

9. Elie Wiesel, *Souls on Fire,* trans. Marion Wiesel (New York: Vintage Books, 1973), p. 52.

10. Nikos Kazantzakis, *Zorba the Greek,* trans. Carl Wildman (New York: Ballantine, 1952), p. 301.

11. W. H. Auden, "In Memory of W. B. Yeats," in *Major Poets: English and American,* ed. Charles Coffin (New York: Harcourt Brace Jovanovich, 1969), p. 537. Subsequent quotations are from this book.

12. Emmanuel Levinas, *Otherwise than Being, or Beyond Essence,* trans. Alphonso Lingis (The Hague: Martinus Nijhoff, 1981), p. 145.

13. Martin Heidegger, *Unterwegs zur Sprache* (Tübingen: Neske, 1959), p. 13. Subsequent quotations are from this book.

14. T. S. Eliot, *Four Quartets* (New York: Harcourt Brace Jovanovich, 1971), p. 59.

15. Michel Foucault, *The Order of Things* (New York: Vintage Books, 1972), p. 93.

16. Elie Wiesel, *The Gates of the Forest,* trans. Frances Frenaye (New York: Holt, Rinehart and Winston, 1966), p. 166.

17. Martin Buber, *The Prophetic Faith,* trans. Carlyle Witton-Davies (New York: Harper & Row, 1960), p. 64.

18. José Ortega y Gasset, *Some Lessons in Metaphysics,* trans. Mildred Adams (New York: W. W. Norton, 1969), p. 31.

19. T. S. Eliot, "Ash Wednesday," in *The Waste Land and Other Poems* (New York: Harcourt Brace Jovanovich, 1962), p. 64.

20. Quoted by Anthony Wilden in Jacques Lacan, *The Language of the Self,* trans. with commentary by Anthony Wilden (Baltimore, Md.: Johns Hopkins University Press, 1968), p. 269.

21. Mikhail Bakhtin, *Estetika slovesnogo tvorchestva* (Moscow, 1979), p. 342. Subsequent quotations are from this book.

22. Elie Wiesel, *Paroles d'étranger* (Paris: Éditions du Seuil, 1982), p. 166.

23. Nikos Kazantzakis, *The Last Temptation of Christ,* trans. P. A. Bien (New York: Bantam Books, 1961), pp. 101–102.

Chapter 2

1. Edmund Husserl, *Phenomenology and the Crisis of Philosophy,* trans. Quentin Lauer (New York: Harper & Row, 1965), p. 110.

2. Norman O. Brown, *Love's Body* (New York: Vintage Books, 1966), p. 195. Subsequent quotations are from this book.

3. Martin Buber, *Ich und Du,* in *Werke,* vol. 1 (Munich: Kösel-Verlag, 1962), p. 103. Subsequent quotations are from this book.

4. Martin Buber, *Daniel,* trans. Maurice Friedman (New York: Holt, Rinehart and Winston, 1964), p. 94.

5. Michel Foucault, *The Order of Things* (New York: Vintage Books, 1973), p. 300. Subsequent quotations are from this book.

6. Søren Kierkegaard, *Training in Christianity,* trans. Walter Lowrie (Princeton, N.J.: Princeton University Press, 1944), p. 201.

7. Denis Diderot, *Oeuvres esthétiques,* ed. Paul Vernière (Paris: Club des Libraires de France, 1959), p. 152.

8. Saint Augustine, *Confessions,* trans. R. S. Pine-Coffin (New York: Penguin Books, 1961), p. 34.

9. William Blake, *Poems and Prophecies,* ed. Max Plowman (New York: E. P. Dutton, 1978), p. 160. Subsequent quotations are from this book.

10. Jean-Paul Sartre, *L'Être et le néant* (Paris: Gallimard, 1943), p. 228.

11. Nicolas Berdyaev, *The Destiny of Man,* trans. Natalie Duddington (New York: Harper & Row, 1960), p. 131.

12. Ludwig Feuerbach, *The Essence of Christianity,* trans. George Eliot (New York: Harper & Row, 1957), p. 242.

13. Martin Heidegger, *Unterwegs zur Sprache* (Tübingen: Neske, 1959), p. 166.

14. Martin Heidegger, *Erläuterungen zu Hölderlins Dichtung,* 2d ed. (Frankfurt am Main: Vittorio Klostermann, 1951), p. 40.

15. Ralph Waldo Emerson, *Selected Writings,* ed. William H. Gilman (New York: New American Library, 1965), p. 316.

16. Jacques Lacan, "Fonction et champ de la parole et du language en psychanalyse," in *Écrits* (Paris: Éditions du Seuil, 1966), p. 138. Subsequent quotatons are from this book.

17. Quoted by Heidegger, *Poetry, Language, Thought,* trans. Albert Hofstadter (New York: Harper & Row, 1971), p. 138.

18. Elie Wiesel, *The Accident,* trans. Anne Borchardt (New York: Avon Books, 1962), pp. 45–46.

19. Elie Wiesel, *Souls on Fire,* trans. Marion Wiesel (New York: Vintage Books, 1973), p. 87.

20. Jacques Derrida, *De la grammatologie* (Paris: Les Éditions de Minuit, 1967), p. 69.

21. José Ortega y Gasset, *Some Lessons in Metaphysics,* trans. Mildred Adams (New York: W. W. Norton, 1969), p. 31.

22. Paul Tillich, *The New Being* (New York: Charles Scribner's Sons, 1955), p. 123. Subsequent quotations are from this book.

23. Martin Buber, *Zwiesprache,* in *Werke,* vol. 1, pp. 187–88.

Chapter 3

1. Frederic Jameson, "Imaginary and Symbolic in Lacan: Marxism, Psychoanalytic Criticism, and the Problem of the Subject," *Yale French Studies* 55-56 (1977): 349. Subsequent quotations are from this article.

2. See Martin Heidegger, *Sein und Zeit,* 2nd ed. (Tübingen: Neimeyer, 1929), pp. 126–30. Subsequent quotations are from this book.

3. Jacques Lacan, *Écrits* (Paris: Éditions du Seuil, 1966), p. 280. Subsequent quotations are from this book.

4. Anthony Wilden, "Lacan and the Discourse of the Other," in Jacques Lacan, *The Language of the Self,* trans. with commentary by Anthony Wilden (Baltimore, Md.: The Johns Hopkins University Press, 1968), p. 200. Subsequent quotations are from this book.

162   THE AFFIRMING FLAME

5. Elie Wiesel, *Célébrations biblique* (Paris: Éditions du Seuil, 1975), p. 15.

6. Mikhail Bakhtin, *Estetika slovesnogo tvorchestva* (Moscow, 1979), p. 109.

7. Robert Con Davis, "The Discourse of Jacques Lacan," in *The Fictional Father: Lacanian Readings of the Text,* ed. Robert Con Davis (Amherst, Mass.: University of Massachusetts Press, 1981), p. 185.

8. Elie Wiesel, *Le mendiant de Jérusalem* (Paris: Éditions du Seuil, 1968), p. 98.

9. Ellie Ragland-Sullivan, "Lacan, Language, and Literary Criticism," *Literary Review* 24 (1981): 570.

10. Stuart Schneiderman, "Afloat with Jacques Lacan," *Diacritics* 1 (1971): 30. Subsequent quotations are from this article.

11. John Brenkman, "The Other and the One: Psychoanalysis, Reading, the *Symposium,*" *Yale French Studies* 55-56 (1977): 434.

12. Shoshana Felman, "To Open the Question," *Yale French Studies* 55-56 (1977): 7.

13. Jane Gallop, *Reading Lacan* (Ithaca, N.Y.: Cornell University Press, 1985), p. 185. Subsequent quotations are from this book.

14. Shoshana Felman, "Beyond Oedipus: The Specimen Story of Psychoanalysis," *Modern Language Notes* 98 (1983): 1045. Subsequent quotations are from this article.

15. Søren Kierkegaard, *Concluding Unscientific Postscript,* trans. David F. Swenson and Walter Lowrie (Princeton, N.J.: Princeton University Press, 1941), pp. 67–68.

16. Søren Kierkegaard, *Point of View for My Work as an Author,* trans. Walter Lowrie (New York: Harper & Row, 1962), p. 110.

17. T. S. Eliot, *Four Quarters* (New York: Harcourt Brace Jovanovich, 1943), p. 26.

18. Søren Kierkegaard, *Fear and Trembling and The Sickness unto Death,* trans. Walter Lowrie (Princeton, N.J.: Princeton University Press, 1968), pp. 114–19.

19. Lev Shestov, *Na vesakh Iova* (Paris: Éditions Franco-Slaves, 1929), pp. 27–93.

20. Albert Camus, *Le mythe de Sisyphe* (Paris: Gallimard, 1942), pp. 167–85.

Chapter 4

1. Fyodor M. Dostoevsky, *Dvoinik,* vol. 1 of *Polnoe sobranie sochinenii* (Leningrad, 1972). Subsequent quotations are from this book.

2. V. G. Belinsky, *Polnoe sobranie sochinenii,* (Moscow, 1955), 9:563.

3. Dyula Kirai, "Kompozitsiya syuzheta romana 'Dvoinik. Priklyucheniya gospodina Golyadkina,'" *Acta Litteraria Academiae Scientiarum Hungaricae* 11 (1969): 364.

4. Dyula Kirai, "Syuzhetny parallizm v romane 'Dvoinik,'" *Studia Slavica* 15 (1969): 246.

5. Natalie Reber, *Studien zur Motiv des Doppelgängers bei Dostoevskij und E. T. A. Hoffman* (Giessen: Wilhelm Schmitz Verlag, 1964), p. 56.

6. Charles C. Hoffmeister, "'William Wilson' and *The Double:* A Freudian Insight," *Coranto* 9 (1974): 26.

7. V. V. Vinogradov, *Evolyutsiya russkogo naturalizma* (Leningrad, 1929), p. 277.

8. Mikhail Bakhtin, *Problemy poetiki Dostoevskogo,* 3d ed. (Moscow, 1972), p. 362. Subsequent quotations are from this book.

9. Jacques Lacan, "Fonction et champ de la parole et du language en psychanalyse," in *Écrits* (Paris: Éditions du Seuil, 1966), p. 257. Subsequent quotations are from this book.

10. Anthony Wilden, "Lacan and the Discourse of the Other," in *The Language of the Self,* trans. with commentary by Anthony Wilden (Baltimore, Md.: Johns Hopkins University Press, 1968), p. 306. Subsequent quotations are from this book.

11. Martin Heidegger, *Sein und Zeit,* 2d ed. (Tübingen: Niemeyer, 1929), p. 337.

12. Jean-Paul Sartre, *L'Être et le néant* (Paris: Gallimard, 1943), p. 276.

13. Michel Foucault, *The Order of Things* (New York: Vintage Books, 1973), p. 49.

14. Jacques Derrida, *De la grammatologie* (Paris: Éditions de Minuit, 1967), pp. 40–41.

15. Quoted by Norman O. Brown, *Love's Body* (New York: Vintage Books, 1966), p. 224.

16. Frederic Jameson, "Imaginary and Symbolic in Lacan: Marxism, Psychoanalytic Criticism, and the Problem of the Subject," *Yale French Studies* 55-56 (1977): 369.

17. Fyodor M. Dostoevsky, *Brat'ya Karamazovy* (Petrozavodsk, 1970), p. 353.

18. Martin Buber, *Ich und Du,* in *Werke,* vol. 1 (Munich: Kösel-Verlag, 1962), p. 90.

19. Fyodor M. Dostoevsky, *Niezdanyi Dostoevsky—Zapiski knizhki i tetradi 1860–1881 gg.,* in *Literaturnoe nasledstvo,* vol. 30, ed. V. R. Shcherbina et al. (Moscow, 1971), p. 529.

Chapter 5

1. Tzvetan Todorov, *Mikhail Bakhtine: Le principe dialogique* (Paris: Éditions du Seuil, 1981), p. 7. Subsequent quotations are from this book.

2. Wayne Booth, "Introduction to Mikhail Bakhtin," in Mikhail Bakhtin, *Problems of Dostoevsky's Poetics*, trans. Caryl Emerson (Minneapolis: University of Minnesota Press, 1984), p. xxv. Subsequent quotations are from this book.

3. Mikhail Bakhtin, "Forms of Time and the Chronotope in the Novel" in *The Dialogic Imagination*, trans. Caryl Emerson and Michael Holquist (Austin: University of Texas Press, 1981), p. 254. Subsequent quotations are from this book.

4. Gary Saul Morson, "Who Speaks for Bakhtin?: A Dialogic Introduction," *Critical Inquiry* 10 (1983): 237.

5. Donald Fanger, "Dostoevsky and Cervantes in the Theory of Bakhtin: the Theory of Bakhtin in Cervantes and Dostoevsky," manuscript.

6. Caryl Emerson, "The Tolstoy Connection in Bakhtin," *Publications of the Modern Language Association* 100 (1985): 70.

7. For a detailed discussion of the word in Bakhtin's works, see David K. Danow, "M. M. Bakhtin's Concept of the Word," *American Journal of Semiotics* 3 (1984): 79–97.

8. Caryl Emerson, "The Outer Word and Inner Speech: Bakhtin, Vygotsky, and the Internalization of Language," *Critical Inquiry* 10 (1983): 247.

9. Mikhail Bakhtin, "Notes from 1970–1971," in *Estetika slovesnogo tvorchestva* (Moscow, 1979), p. 357. Subsequent quotations are from this book.

10. V. N. Voloshinov, *Marksizm i filosofiya yaazyka*, 2d ed. (Leningrad, 1930), p. 18. There is some argument as to whether Voloshinov or Bakhtin is actually the author of this work.

11. Martin Heidegger, *Poetry, Language, Thought*, trans. Albert Hofstadter (New York: Harper & Row, 1971), p. 108.

12. For a discussion of the importance of the relation between self and other in Bakhtin's writings, see Michael Holquist, "Answering as Authoring: Mikhail Bakhtin's Trans-Linguistics," *Critical Inquiry* 10 (1983): 307–19. Subsequent quotations are from this article.

13. Jacques Lacan, *The Language of the Self*, trans. with notes and commentary by Anthony Wilden (Baltimore, Md.: Johns Hopkins University Press, 1968), p. 9.

14. Michel Foucault, *The Order of Things* (New York: Vintage Books, 1968), p. 305.

15. Martin Heidegger, *Unterwegs zur Sprache* (Tübingen: Neske, 1959), p. 32.

16. Holquist discusses Bakhtin's religious affiliations in "the Politics of Representation" in *Allegory and Representation: Selected Papers from the English Institute, 1979–1980*, ed. Stephen J. Greenblatt (Baltimore, Md.: Johns Hopkins University Press, 1981), pp. 171–76.

17. Martin Buber, *I and Thou*, trans. Walter Kaufmann (New York: Charles Scribner's Sons, 1970), p. 89.

Chapter 6

1. See Martin Buber, *The Legend of the Baal Shem,* trans. Maurice Friedman (New York: Shocken Books, 1969), pp. 52–53.

2. Martin Buber, *Die Erzühlungen der Chassidim,* in *Werke,* vol. 3 (Munich: Kösel-Verlag, 1963), p. 168. Subsequent quotations are from this book.

3. Martin Buber, *Die chassidische Botschaft,* in *Werke,* vol. 3, p. 894. Subsequent quotations are from this book.

4. Elie Wiesel, *Souls on Fire,* trans. Marion Wiesel (New York: Vintage Books, 1973), p. 257. Subsequent quotations are from this book.

5. Elie Wiesel, *Somewhere a Master,* trans. Marion Wiesel (New York: Summit Books, 1982), p. 191. Subsequent quotations are from this book.

6. Martin Buber, *Mein Weg zum Chassidismus,* in *Werke,* vol. 3, p. 962.

7. Martin Buber, *Vom Leben der Chassidim,* in *Werke,* vol. 3, p. 37. Subsequent quotations are from this book.

8. Elie Wiesel, *The Gates of the Forest,* trans. Frances Frenaye (New York: Holt, Rinehart and Winston, 1966), p. 166. Subsequent quotations are from this book.

9. Abraham Joshua Heschel, *A Passion for Truth* (New York: Farrar, Straus and Giroux, 1973), p. 249.

10. Martin Buber, *Die Frage an den Einzelnen,* in *Werke,* vol. 1, p. 222.

11. Martin Buber, *Reden über Erziehung,* in *Werke,* vol. 1, p. 823. Subsequent quotations are from this book.

12. Elie Wiesel, *One Generation After* (New York: Pocket Books, 1970), p. 241. Subsequent quotations are from this book.

13. Martin Buber, *Rabbi Nachman von Bratzlaw,* in *Werke,* vol. 3, p. 902.

14. Elie Wiesel, *Le mendiant de Jérusalem* (Paris: Éditions du Seuil, 1968), p. 122. Subsequent quotations are from this book.

15. Martin Buber, *Der Chassidismus und der abendländische Mensch,* in *Werke,* vol. 3, p. 947.

16. Martin Buber, *Ich und Du,* in *Werke,* vol. 1, p. 131. Subsequent quotations are from this book.

17. Elie Wiesel, *Legends of Our Time* (New York: Avon Books, 1968), p. 126.

18. Elie Wiesel, *The Oath* (New York: Avon Books, 1973), p. 88. Subsequent quotations are from this book.

19. Elie Wiesel, *The Town Beyond the Wall,* trans. Stephen Becker (New York: Vintage Books, 1964), p. 188.

20. Elie Wiesel, *Four Hasidic Masters* (Notre Dame, Ind.: University of Notre Dame Press, 1978), p. 122. Subsequent quotations are from this book.

21. Elie Wiesel, *Célébration biblique* (Paris: Éditions du Seuil, 1975), p. 15.

22. Elie Wiesel, *The Trial of God,* trans. Marion Wiesel (New York: Random House, 1979), p. 49.

23. Elie Wiesel, *The Accident,* trans. Anna Borchardt (New York: Avon Books, 1962), p. 81.

24. Elie Wiesel, *Five Biblical Portraits* (Notre Dame, Ind.: University of Notre Dame Press, 1981), p. 2.

25. Martin Buber, *Das Problem des Menschen,* in *Werke,* vol. 1, p. 363.

26. Elie Wiesel, *Night,* trans. Stella Rodway (New York: Hill and Wang, 1961), pp. 70–71.

Chapter 7

1. Elie Wiesel, *A Jew Today,* trans. Marion Wiesel (New York: Random House, 1978), pp. 178–79. Subsequent quotations are from this book.

2. Elie Wiesel, *The Oath* (New York: Avon Books, 1973), p. 132. Subsequent quotations are from this book.

3. Elie Wiesel, *The Town Beyond the Wall,* trans. Stephen Becker (New York: Avon Books, 1964), p. 94. Subsequent quotations are from this book.

4. Elie Wiesel, *Night,* trans. Stella Rodway (New York: Hill and Wang, 1961), pp. 70–71.

5. Elie Wiesel, *One Generation After* (New York: Pocket Books, 1965), p. 124. Subsequent quotations are from this book.

6. Elie Wiesel, *Célébration biblique* (Paris: Éditions du Seuil, 1975), p. 57. Subsequent quotations are from this book.

7. Elie Wiesel, *Le mendiant de Jérusalem* (Paris: Éditions du Seuil, 1969), p. 208. Subsequent quotations are from this book.

8. Elie Wiesel, *Ani Maamin,* trans. Marion Wiesel (New York: Random House, 1973), pp. 27, 29. Subsequent quotations are from this book.

9. Elie Wiesel, *Dawn,* trans. Frances Frenaye (New York: Hill and Wang, 1961), pp. 68–69.

10. Elie Wiesel, *The Testament,* trans. Marion Wiesel (New York: Summit Books, 1981), pp. 307–308. Subsequent quotations are from this book.

11. Elie Wiesel, *Somewhere a Master,* trans. Marion Wiesel (New York: Summit Books, 1982), p. 106.

12. Elie Wiesel, *The Gates of the Forest,* trans. Frances Frenaye (New York: Holt, Rinehart and Winston, 1966), p. 14. Subsequent quotations are from this book.

13. Elie Wiesel, *Zalmen, or The Madness of God,* adapted for the stage by Marion Wiesel (New York: Random House, 1974), p. 4. Subsequent quotations are from this book.

14. Elie Wiesel, *Legends of Our Time* (New York: Avon Books, 1968), pp. 223–24.

15. Elie Wiesel, *Four Hasidic Masters* (Notre Dame, Ind.: University of Notre Dame Press, 1978), p. 123.

Chapter 8

1. Elie Wiesel, *The Testament,* trans. Marion Wiesel (New York: Summit Books, 1981), p. 72. Subsequent quotations are from this book.

2. Elie Wiesel, *The Oath* (New York: Avon Books, 1973), p. 196. Subsequent quotations are from this book.

3. For further observations on the significance of silence in Elie Wiesel's works, see Ted L. Estess, *Elie Wiesel* (New York: Frederick Ungar, 1980), pp. 99–100; see also Terrence Des Pres, "The Authority of Silence in Elie Wiesel's Art" in *Confronting the Holocaust,* ed. Alvin H. Rosenfeld and Irving Greenberg (Bloomington, Ind.: Indiana University Press, 1978), pp. 49–57. Subsequent quotations are from this book.

4. Elie Wiesel, *Somewhere a Master,* trans. Marion Wiesel (New York: Summit Books, 1982), p. 201. Subsequent quotations are from this book.

5. Martin Buber, *Daniel,* trans. Maurice Friedman (New York: Holt, Rinehart and Winston, 1964), p. 142.

6. See Harry A. Long, *Personal and Family Names* (Detroit: Gale Research, 1968), p. 37.

7. Elie Wiesel, *A Beggar in Jerusalem,* trans. Lily Edelman and Elie Wiesel (New York: Random House, 1970), p. 11.

8. Elie Wiesel, *One Generation After* (New York: Pocket Books, 1970), p. 214.

9. Elie Wiesel, *The Town beyond the Wall,* trans. Stephen Becker (New York: Avon Books, 1964), p. 187.

10. Elie Wiesel, *The Accident,* trans. Anne Borchardt (New York: Avon Books, 1962), p. 81.

11. Ludwig Feuerbach, *The Essence of Christianity,* trans. George Eliot (New York: Harper & Row, 1957), p. 53.

Select Bibliography

Bakhtin, Mikhail. *The Dialogic Imagination*. Trans. Caryl Emerson and Michael Holquist. Austin: University of Texas Press, 1981.

―――. *Estetika slovesnogo tvorchestva*. Moscow, 1979.

―――. *Problems of Dostoevsky's Poetics*. Trans. Caryl Emerson. Minneapolis: University of Minnesota Press, 1984.

Barthes, Roland. *The Pleasure of the Text*. Trans. Richard Miller. New York: Hill and Wang, 1973.

―――. *The Rustle of Language*. Trans. Richard Howard. New York: Hill and Wang, 1985.

―――. *S/Z*. Trans. Richard Miller. New York: Hill and Wang, 1974.

Bultman, Rudolph, and Karl Jaspers. *Myth and Christianity*. Trans. Norbert Gutman. New York: Noonday, 1958.

Burke, Kenneth. *Language as Symbolic Action*. Berkeley: University of California Press, 1966.

―――. *The Rhetoric of Religion: Studies in Logology*. Berkeley: University of California Press, 1970.

Dawson, Christopher. *Religion and Culture*. New York: Meridian, 1958.

DeMan, Paul. *Blindness and Insight*. New York: Oxford University Press, 1971.

Derrida, Jacques. *Of Grammatology*. Trans. Gayatri Chakravorty Spivak. Baltimore, Md.: Johns Hopkins University Press, 1976.

Foucault, Michel. *The Order of Things*. New York: Vintage Books, 1970.

Frye, Northrop. *The Anatomy of Criticism*. Princeton, N.J.: Princeton University Press, 1957.

———. *The Critical Path*. Bloomington: Indiana University Press, 1971.

Gardner, Dame H. *Religion and Literature*. New York: Oxford University Press, 1983.

Glicksburg, Charles, *Literature and Religion: A Study in Conflict*. Westport, Conn.: Greenwood, 1960.

Handelman, Susan. *The Slayers of Moses*. Albany: State University of New York Press, 1982.

Hartman, Geoffrey. *Criticism in the Wilderness*. New Haven, Conn.: Yale University Press, 1980.

———. *The Fate of Reading and Other Essays*. Chicago: University of Chicago Press, 1975.

———. *Saving the Text: Literature/Derrida/Philosophy*. Baltimore, Md.: Johns Hopkins University Press, 1982.

Heidegger, Martin. *On the Way to Language*. New York: Harper & Row, 1982.

———. *Poetry, Language, Thought*. Trans. Albert Hofstadter. New York: Harper & Row, 1971.

Jameson, Frederic. *The Prison-House of Language*. Princeton, N.J.: Princeton University Press, 1972.

Lacan, Jacques. *The Language of the Self*. Trans. with commentary by Anthony Wilden. Baltimore, Md.: Johns Hopkins University Press, 1968.

Lynch, William F. *Christ and Apollo: The Dimensions of the Literary Imagination*. New York: New American Library, 1960.

May, Rollo, ed. *Symbolism in Religion and Literature*. New York: George Braziller, 1961.

Milosz, Czeslaw. *The Witness of Poetry*. Cambridge, Mass.: Harvard University Press, 1983.

Mulder, John R., ed. *Religion and Literature: The Convergence of Approaches*. Baltimore, Md.: Scholars Press, 1983.

Ong, Walter J. *Interfaces of the Word*. Ithaca, N.Y.: Cornell University Press, 1982.

————. *The Presence of the Word*. New York: Simon and Schuster, 1970.

Ricoeur, Paul. *The Conflict of Interpretation: Essays on Hermeneutics*. Evanston, Ill.: Northwestern University Press, 1974.

————. *The Rule of Metaphor*. Toronto: University of Toronto Press, 1977.

Schneidau, Herbert. *Sacred Discontent: The Bible in Western Tradition*. Berkeley: University of California Press, 1976.

Index

Abraham: 34, 117, 125, 138, 140, 155
Absalom: 137
Abyss, the: 7–8, 29, 43, 95, 108; and the Word, 96
Adam: 40, 104
Aesthetics: 23–25, 92
Aharon of Karlin: 110
Auerbach, Erich: 27
Auschwitz, Poland: 128
Author, the: 88; and the hero, 82–85, 91–92

Baal Shem Tov: 7, 93–94, 99, 101, 107, 109, 110
Belle âme: 67–68
Belzec, Poland: 103
Bhagavad Gita: 15
Bible: 5, 15, 117
Bloom, Harold: 5

Cain: 121
Culler, Jonathan: 157

Dante: 117
Das Man, or the They: 38ff., 51–52, 57, 64–65

Davhar: 5, 10, 12, 22; *see also* logos, the Word
David, King: 137, 144
David of Lelov: 101
Death: 6, 49–50, 54–55, 67, 102, 106, 112–13, 118–20, 122–23, 133, 143–44

Faith: 29, 111, 126, 150, 153
Father, the: 70, 131–32, 136–40
Freedom: 81–82, 143
Freud, Sigmund: 37, 59
Freudianism: 23, 31, 46, 53, 59

Gide, André: 135
Goethe, Johann Wolfgang: 48, 55, 72
Gogol, Nikolai: 89
Guilt: 111, 137: *see also* sin

Hegel, Georg Wilhelm: 37
Hersh, Rebbe: 7
Hosea: 9

Isaac: 138
Isaiah: 9, 10, 35, 117, 125
Israel of Rizhin: 99

Jacob: 138
Jeremiah: 9
Jerusalem, Israel: 149
Jesus: 21–22, 28, 155
Joel: 9
Joy: 4, 8, 18, 107–108, 127, 141
Joyce, James: 48, 88
Judaic tradition: 5, 12, 21–22

Kafka, Franz: 55
Koran: 15

Laughter: 81, 83ff., 143
Law, the: 70, 137
Leib, Moshe of Sassov: 99, 127
Logos: 10, 21–22, 34–35, 78–79,
    153; and literature, 23–27; *see
    also davhar,* the Word
Love: 4, 8–9, 22, 25–27, 49–50,
    71, 100, 102, 127, 150–51, 153,
    156–57; and presence, 108–10
Lublin, Poland: 103

Madness: 62, 65, 71, 127–29
Maggid of Mezeritch: 95, 97, 99,
    107
Majdanek, Poland: 103
Mallarmé, Stéphane: 36
Marxism: 23, 31, 53
Meaning: 11–15, 26–27, 81–82,
    88–89, 101, 154; and time, 14,
    89–90
Mendl, Menahem of Kotzk: 105
Mendl, Menahem of Vitebsk: 98
Milton, John: 117
Murder: 120–21, 132
Myth: 4, 81

Nahman of Bratzlav: 98–99, 107
Naphtali of Ropshitz: 102–103
Nietzsche, Friedrich: 36, 155

Open, the: 7–8, 51, 108ff.
Other, the (capital *O*): 11, 13,
    43ff., 53–54, 61, 68–71; and
    truth, 46–48, 86; *see also*
    the Third
other, the (lowercase *o*): 43ff.; 61–
    62, 71, 80–81, 91; and the self,
    64–68

Paraclete: 122–23, 148
Passion, movement of: 105–11
Paul, the Apostle: 24
Philo of Alexandria: 21
Pinhas of Koretz: 103, 110
Plato: 14, 21
Polyglossia: 80ff.
Prayer: 12, 71, 97–98
Presence: 10, 25, 32–33, 48ff.,
    52–55, 94, 96–98, 155; and
    truth, 86–90; between I and
    Thou, 100–105, 130

Rawicz, Piotr: 128
Redemption: 35, 70, 107, 118,
    122–25, 128–29, 133, 139–40,
    141–42, 155–56
Responsibility: 12, 51–54, 92, 96,
    153–54
Rilke, Rainer Maria: 8, 30

Seer of Lublin: 103, 105–106, 111
Self, the: and the word, 38–43; and
    critical response, 43–50; and
    truth, 50–55; structure of, 60–
    64; and the other, 64–68; in re-
    lation to itself, 84–85, 129–32,
    138–39
Shakespeare, William: 23, 25, 55
Shekhina: 94, 97
Shmelke of Nikolsburg: 110

Silence: 54, 69ff., 122, 134, 142,
144–46, 155
Sin: 111–12; *see also* guilt
Soul: 24, 91–92, 98
Spirit: 10, 13–16, 22ff., 29, 35,
41–42, 67, 91–97, 106, 157; in
the I-Thou relation, 104–105;
see also the Word

Talmud: 15, 125
Tao te-ching: 15
Targums: 21–22
Teradion, Hanina ben R.: 15
They, the: *see Das Man*
Third, the: 11, 47, 86–88, 91; *see
also* the Other
Time: 6, 79–80, 89–90, 94; and
meaning, 89–90; and eternity,
107, 109
Torah: 15, 129

Truth: 11, 27, 46, 48, 83, 156; and
literature, 27–31; born in the
Word, 47, 50–55; and presence,
86–90

Word, the: 4–14, 21ff., 62, 87–88,
95–100; in the critical response,
31–36, 52–55; as the language
of the self, 38–43, 62, 64, 153;
and truth, 50–55; and judgment,
68–71; and discourse in the
novel, 78–81; and spirit, 22, 25,
91–92, 104, 152–54; and the
quest for the Messiah, 143–49;
see also davhar, logos
Writing: 5–6, 67

Yeats, William Butler: 8
Yitzhak of Vorki: 111